LIGHT RELIEF

Twenty sketches to help you explore the Bible through drama

Richard Cole

A Bible Society Creative Handbook

BIBLE SOCIETY
Stonehill Green, Westlea, Swindon SN5 7DY, England.

Unless otherwise stated, quotations from the Bible are from the Good News Bible, published by the Bible Societies/Collins, © American Bible Society, New York, 1966, 1971, 1976.

The quotation from the Bible on page 51 is from the New Revised Standard Version, © 1989, by the Division of Christian Education of the National Council of Churches of Christ in the USA and used by permission.

First published 1991.

British Library Cataloguing in Publication Data
Cole, Richard
  Light Relief: sketches to help explore the bible through drama
  1. Christianity. Scriptures
  I. Title
  220.6

ISBN 0 564 05995 1

Important
The dramatic material in this book may be performed free of charge, providing that the following conditions are met:
1. That the performance is by an amateur group
2. For performance before a live non-paying audience
3. That the author of the work performed is properly credited in any programme or hand-out
4. The above does not confirm any right to perform any of the material in the book on television, radio, film, video or audio recording, or in any other way except as stated above.

For performances that do not fall within these conditions, you are requested to contact Bible Society, at the address above, to make appropriate arrangements.

Please note: the permission granted above applies only in respect of performances. No part of this book may be copied without specific permission from the publisher. It therefore follows that unless you have obtained such permission (for which a charge may be made), you should purchase sufficient copies of the book to enable you to rehearse any dramatic piece from it.

Bible Societies exist to provide resources for Bible distribution and use. Bible Society in England and Wales (BFBS) is a member of the United Bible Societies, an international partnership working in over 180 countries. Their common aim is to reach all people with the Bible, or some part of it, in a language they can understand and at a price they can afford. Parts of the Bible have now been translated into approximately 1,800 languages. Bible Societies aim to help every church at every point where it uses the Bible. You are invited to share in this work by your prayers and gifts. The Bible Society in your country will be very happy to provide details of its activity.

Foreword

I am very happy to commend this book of sketches. Richard Cole has prefaced the sketches with a few pages of helpful hints, such as "Cringe Intros" – how not to introduce the sketches! They have been performed within the Solent area by the Lightswitch gospel team, and so have been tried and tested for effectiveness.

Light Relief contains material that would be useful for a wide range of occasions, and the sketches cater for varying age groups – both in production and for the audience. The sketches are humorous, and use everyday life situations to explore and bring home the relevance of Christian teaching. *Light Relief* is a superb resource book for any church.

+ **John Southampton**

Acknowledgements

This collection of sketches would never have been put together without the love and help of my wife, family and friends.

The Lightswitch team – Steve, Lainie, Ruth, Stuart, Sarah, Brian, Bev, Mike, Aaron, Helen, Jo, Barry and Sandra – egged me on and, more importantly, told me when I was writing rubbish! Many of the sketches in this book are a result of consumer testing by this talented bunch and I owe them a great debt of gratitude.

Brian Robinson originally wrote *Tempting Mortals* and I originally wrote *Going Back*. We then re-wrote each other's sketches and so the results are two co-written pieces. I wish to acknowledge Brian's efforts in this book which bears my name.

My wife, Edwina, and my three children have had to put up with hours of keyboard-tapping from the study and grunts from Dad when he became too absorbed in the work! The hours of rehearsal and performance put in by the Lightswitch team prompted my eldest daughter to suggest I give it all up for Lent!

Contents

Introduction	1
Ribbons	4
Come on down	7
News at Pentecost	13
Scraggle	16
Going back	20
Garments	25
Perfect timing	30
A pair of trainers	35
Sam	40
Blinder	43
I stand at the door	48
The old bag	52
Armour getting	56
A select group	62
Temptation	65
Drawing conclusions	67
Faithing reality	73
Tempting mortals	78
Knock three times	83
Money man	87
Suggested reading	91

Introduction

This collection of sketches has been written and tested over a number of years by Lightswitch – a Christian group from the Solent area who specialize in drama and music presentations. The group has been seen (and heard!) in many churches, schools conferences, youth groups and outdoor events over the past five years.

The sketches will work for you if you are willing to give them a go and put in some rehearsal time. You will soon become aware that they have large slices of comedy running through them. They could be just what is needed for a school assembly, youth night, church service or meeting and be the way that reaches those people that other ways don't.

Using Light Relief

Having decided on the sketch or sketches you are going to use at a particular event – be it a formal service, lively youth event, social gathering or whatever – you may be asking yourselves whether the choice is suitable for the age of audience. *Light Relief* contains material that is appropriate for people of all ages and Lightswitch certainly found that the sketches could relate to any audience that they met. Some, such as *Ribbons* or *Garments*, give a particular opportunity to involve children while others might require a little more depth of thought. *Perfect Timing* and *Money Man* might be more suitable for an older group for this reason.

The selection of sketches here also covers a wide range of material for different occasions and you should be able to find something appropriate for a special time or event.

Introducing sketches
If the sketches you use form part of a package of drama, music, readings, etc., then they will require careful linking, and you will need to decide who is going to link such fragments together and involve them in the rehearsal wherever possible.

Using music
When you are thinking about the presentation of these pieces

it is worth remembering the effect that a piece of music or a chorus has in drama. Indeed, many of the sketches in this book give examples of when music would be appropriate. You will not always want the audience to applaud your efforts and, having created an atmosphere in something like *Come On Down*, you will want to extend that dramatic moment further and lead them on to another thought. Unlike curtains and lighting changes, music is usually easily available and can clearly show when a sketch is over and something new is about to happen.

School work

In schools or colleges there is often a need to capture the attention of the audience by using drama. Some Scripture passages commonly used in assemblies are here in sketch form. They are particularly good for youth work. For example:

Armour Getting	*A Select Group*
Blinder	*Come on Down*
Faithing Reality	*Knock Three Times*
Garments	*Ribbons*
A Pair of Trainers	*Scraggle*
Sam	*Tempting Mortals*
Temptation	

Lightswitch have often used the material alongside talks and readings as well as with their music presentation. Look at the talents that your group have to offer and fit them and the material into a programme that works best for you.

Preparation

Different kinds of preparation are needed. It is important for there to be prayer and thought when this material is being used, as well as for practical arrangements to be made.

If you are using *Garments* or *Ribbons* with children, then it will be a good idea to have a trial run. Get members of your group or family to take the children's parts and see what reactions you get from them. This will give you, as leader, a clue as to what to expect when you get strangers to participate. You won't be prepared for all the reactions that children will give but at least you'll be expecting certain responses.

Talking to yourself

Monologues, such as *Sam* or *Scraggle*, require a particular skill too. Don't expect any member of your drama group just to be able to perform one of these. They require rehearsal and direction. The performer will then be able to gauge when to pause, when to anticipate a reaction, when to emphasize certain points. Although a lot can be achieved in front of a mirror or with a tape recorder, honest, constructive criticism from others cannot be beaten.

Practical problems

It is always worth finding out as much about the venue and physical situation beforehand. How many ways in/out? Where are the electric sockets? Will there be any other groups there too? (Useful to know if space is limited or if resources can be shared.) For sketches like *The Old Bag* it would be good to know if there are any dangers on the "stage" – gratings for coins to fall down, steps to negotiate etc.

Props

At the beginning of each sketch is a list of props. You do not always have to have everything that is listed – if you cannot get hold of something then feel free to improvise!

Then what?

If you use these sketches then you can be prepared for some reaction! It may come in the form of hecklers in the street who are probably best dealt with by the non-actors of your group. Reaction is usually positive though, and you and your group can expect to make many new friends through the messages of the sketches. It is my hope that the sketches you use will not just receive polite comments like "that was good", "I liked that funny one you did" and so on. Strive to make the drama effective so that reactions are more in the style of "I enjoyed that sketch, it meant something to me."

You and your audience will recognize many of the scenes within this book and if people recognize themselves then so much the better!

Ribbons

Bible basis: Some of the events from Palm Sunday to Easter
Mark 15.6–10; 15.11–14, 24–37; 16.1–7

Characters: NARRATOR/LEADER
A CROWD
JESUS (can be played by different people)

Properties: Bright coloured ribbons/strips of material.

"Can you do some drama for us this Easter please?"
"What sort?"
"Something that involves the children?"
"How many?"
"At least fifty but it might be eighty . . . last year . . ."
"How many?!"
"The leaders will help as well . . . we'd like to join in . . ."
"Got any ribbons?"

That is how the sketch began. Then it grew and grew. At an Easter workshop for our church we told the story in short episodes, had various activities (making Easter gardens, stained glass windows, movable donkeys etc.), songs, choruses and so on, then brought the morning to a close with this piece of drama called *Ribbons*.

Use the script as a guideline and be prepared to improvise to the actual reactions of the crowd. You may prefer to rehearse each section and then present the whole piece at a suitable point in the proceedings. The crucifixion part needs to be worked out by the few involved and should not be seen by the audience before they have done their part.

The bright coloured ribbons were very cheap and effective. It was interesting to see the children (and adults) going home with their bits of ribbon and talking about their Easter experience to those they met.

Provide the CROWD *with a ribbon or strip of material each. The crowd copy the actions of the* LEADER.

LEADER: When Jesus entered Jerusalem upon a donkey

he was greeted by a huge crowd who waved palm leaves as he rode by.

(Everyone now waves their ribbons and cheers as Jesus passes by. It is good if you can get the crowd to react to the movements of others. For example, the people on the left should stand, wave and then sit down. As soon as they have sat, the next row repeat that action and so on across the whole assembly. Thus a wave is created – with a little coaxing from the leader no doubt!)

LEADER: Hosanna! they cried. *(Encourage others to join in the shout. Repeat as necessary to create the right atmosphere.)*

LEADER: But the crowd changed and the shouts of Hosanna changed to a cry of a different kind.

(Everyone in the CROWD *now holds both ends of the ribbon and makes a snapping sound by pulling it tight.* JESUS *stands amid the crowd. A few of the* CROWD *whip him with their ribbons. It is possible to get a cracking sound from a ribbon but a slow movement with the ribbon being dragged across the body is also effective.*

The LEADER *starts a quiet call of "crucify" and encourages the others to join in. This will build to an intense shout as* JESUS *dies on the cross – he stands in front of the crowd with arms stretched out on a length of material or ribbon. It is held at either end by others. As the shout reaches its climax the material is pulled tight and* JESUS *hangs on the "cross".)*

LEADER: His side was pierced.

(A few of the ribbon-carriers drape their ribbons over the body.)

LEADER: Jesus died and was buried.

(Stillness everywhere as the cross is lowered and JESUS *lies on the ground.)*

LEADER: The powers of darkness were over the land and the people were imprisoned by their sins.

(The CROWD *hold their hands up slowly showing the ribbon to be wrapped around their wrists like handcuffs.)*

LEADER: But on the third day he rose again.

*(*JESUS *gets up and shakes loose the ribbons. The others watch, still manacled.)*

LEADER: He died to set people free.

(At this the CROWD *who have been watching start a whispered "He's alive . . . He has risen".*

As this slowly builds to a climax each ribbon is loosened and falls to the ground. JESUS *could also move around the group taking the ribbons away from them (symbolically freeing them from their sins). A song such as "Clap your hands, all you people" finishes the piece well. It has to be lively, catchy (you don't want books here!) and light. The sort of song to make you want to dance and rejoice.)*

Come on down

Bible basis: The watchful servant
Luke 12.35–40

Characters: BEN FORESIGHT, the jovial TV compère
TESSA CASE, first contestant
SHAMUS BOND, second contestant
ALEC SMART, third contestant
ANNOUNCER, (not seen)
HOSTESSES et al

Scene: The stage of a TV quiz show, full of the "glamour" associated with such programmes

Properties: Cards indicating how audience should react
All the usual TV trimmings for a brash show

Sound FX: Noise of buzzer
Noise of clock

Music: "Razzamatazz"
James Bond type
Something sinister

We do not know just when or how Jesus will return and the contestants in this brash TV game show have their own ways of causing chaos before that event.

If you can get a good musician to play suitable music to accompany the sketch then do so. At the end of the sketch you need to create an atmosphere which sends shivers down people's spines and makes them realize the importance of being at peace with God now.

There must be plenty of razzamatazz music throughout. It would add greatly to the sketch if the audience have been warmed up beforehand and are ready to join in with all the catchphrases that are trotted out. Sick bags may be needed! So, before starting, tell the audience the reactions you want – use cards as prompts if need be – and get them to cheer, boo, applaud, chant "Come on down", etc.

Razzamatazz music etc. for the opening during which the three contenders could be summoned from the audience ("Come on down").

VOICE: And here's your host for the evening . . . Ben
Foresight!
(Enter BEN *– obnoxious in the extreme.)*

BEN: Good evening, good evening, good evening! If
you play your cards right you'll come on down
for a devil of a good time. So it's three-two-one
and a starter for ten – just shout out "Bingo" to
Uncle Ben! *(Razzamatazz music etc. and shouts of
"Bingo" as* BEN *moves to first contestant –* TESSA
CASE.*)* Can we have our first contestant please
. . . Welcome to "Come on Down" . . . your
name please?

TESSA: Tessa Case.

BEN: What a great name. Isn't that a great name?
Have you had it long?

TESSA: All my life!

BEN: All her life! Wow, what a comedian! And tell
me, Trudy . . .

TESSA: Tessa!

BEN: Tessa of course . . . just tessa-ting you out . . .
what a memory! Tell me Tessa, my love, where
do you come from?

TESSA: Down below.

BEN: Down below. Wow! Great! Terrific! We have a
contestant from down below, ladies and
gentlemen, boys and girls. Well, you know
what Uncle Ben always says *(With* AUDIENCE *help)*
. . . better the devil you know!
(Razzamatazz music etc.)

BEN: And tell me Tessa, what prize are you after?

TESSA: Well, Ben, I'd rather like to cause chaos on earth
if I'm good enough.

BEN: Oh, you're good enough, my love, but are you
bad enough! Shall we let her try?

AUDIENCE: Yes!

BEN: Come on down then and go for your prize! Will
Tessa Case cause chaos on earth? Let's find out
as she plays *(With* AUDIENCE*)* "Come on Down"!
(Razzamatazz music etc.)

BEN: Take your time now. Four simple questions and

you could be on that earth causing chaos. We wish you well. Are you ready?

TESSA: Yes.

BEN: OK. Question one. Who made the flowers?

TESSA: *(After thinking)* Pass.

BEN: Never mind. Question two. Who made the stars?

TESSA: Pass.

BEN: Come on Tessa you can still do it. Number three . . . who made the birds in the sky?

TESSA: Pass.

BEN: OK. Last question . . . we're really rooting for you, Tessa. We really want you to cause chaos on earth. Last question, Tessa. Who made you?

TESSA: *(Quiet)* Pass.

(A buzzer sounds to denote the end.)

BEN: Well, bad luck. What can I say? You don't make the grade, you're a failure, you're on the trash heap of life . . . so . . . ?

BEN &
AUDIENCE: Go away!!

(The HOSTESSES take TESSA unceremoniously away and lead on the new contestant – SHAMUS BOND. Razzamatazz, with James Bond theme if possible.)

BEN: Well, and who might you be?

BOND: Bond. Shamus Bond.

BEN: Well I hope the disaster of the last contestant didn't put you off too much.

BOND: I was a little shaken . . .

BEN: But not stirred, eh?

BOND: All part of my training, Ben.

BEN: And how has the devil trained you, Shamus?

BOND: He's done a good job. I'm confident that I can cause more chaos on earth than any other devil you care to mention.

BEN: That's what we like to hear, Shamus, or can I call you devil 0 7?!

BOND: I like it. Let's play.

BEN: What a contender, ladies and gentlemen. He just can't wait to start so shall we let him?

AUDIENCE: Yes!

BEN: OK. Then let's play *(With* AUDIENCE*)* . . . "Come on Down"!

(Razzamatazz music etc.)

BEN: OK Shamus, here's what you have to do to get onto earth and cause chaos. I want you to answer these questions – the sort that you might come face to face with each day. We wish you well then . . . start the clock.

(Clock sound starts in background.)

BEN: Which is the most incredible . . . ? Do you understand the question?

BOND: Yes I do.

BEN: OK. Which is the most incredible? Your watch or your heart?

BOND: My watch or my heart? Well I'd say . . . my . . . my heart.

BEN: I'm afraid that's the wrong answer for you to give. If you give glory to God in your heart you will never cause chaos on earth. Never mind – try this one: could a dictionary be caused by an explosion in a printing works? Let me repeat it for you . . . could a dictionary be caused by an explosion in a printing works?

BOND: Yes. I suppose it's just possible.

BEN: Wrong again I'm afraid. Saying "it's just possible" makes it very hard to convince people that creation happened by a chance explosion in space. Yet if you don't believe in God then you can't believe that he did it.

BOND: I'm sorry. I thought I'd do better than this.

BEN: Thousands . . . no . . . millions of people fall down on that one.

BOND: What? They believe in creation being a chance explosion in space?

BEN: Oh yes – they believe the world happened by accident.

BOND: That's incredible.

BEN: Incredible or not I'm afraid we have to say goodbye but thanks for playing *(With* AUDIENCE*)*

"Come on Down"!

(BOND *is escorted away and* ALEC SMART *comes in. The whole atmosphere needs to change now. A sinister piece of music in the distance, a change of set all help.* BEN's *mood certainly changes and he is not as confident as he was with previous contestants.* SMART *is quietly in command.*)

BEN: Well, looky here. Another contestant ready to cause chaos on earth if he can pass this final test. What is your name, sir?

ALEC: Alec Smart.

BEN: A great name for a great bloke, Alec. Are you ready for the set of questions?

ALEC: Quite ready.

BEN: Oh you are so cool, so calm, I think you might just do it. Shall we let him try, audience?

AUDIENCE: Yes!

BEN: All right then, for Alec Smart, come on down!
(*Razzamatazz music etc.*)

BEN: Here we go then, Alec. Do you have a way of causing chaos on earth?

ALEC: Yes. I do.

BEN: Is it a nuclear bomb, Alec?

ALEC: No. I've got a better way.

BEN: Is it a killer disease?

ALEC: No. It's more destructive. The cure is harder to find.

BEN: Hey, ladies and gentlemen, what have we got here? I'd say he's in with a devil of a good chance. Come on . . . tell us more . . .

ALEC: Not yet.

BEN: Oh, come on – we want to know. You're not going to tell them there's no God?

ALEC: Not exactly. It's about Jesus' second coming.

BEN: You're going to stop it?!

ALEC: Oh no – it'll happen.

BEN: Well how will you cause so much chaos then? It's been said for years that Jesus will come again . . . like a thief in the night . . . when it's least expected. Everyone's been told to get ready.

ALEC: That's right.

BEN: Then how will you cause such chaos?

ALEC: I'll just tell them they've got plenty of time left.

BEN: Plenty of time?

ALEC: Yes. (*Softly with a hint of menace*) That's right . . .
you've got plenty of time.
(*Razzamatazz music changes to a haunting, discordant sound – plenty of reverb and echo if possible. A chilling climax to the sketch.*)

News at Pentecost

Bible basis: The events at Pentecost
Acts 2

Characters: A; REPORTER
B; PETER
C; MARY
D; WOMAN
E; MAN

Music: Appropriate music

When we used the sketch we split it into three parts by using hymns, choruses etc. between each section. Time passing could be shown in other ways – change of lighting, freeze then unfreeze and so on.

The sketch captures the confusion of those days when Jesus was here, then gone, then alive again, then finally gone. Many people find this extremely hard to grasp. This sketch might shed some light on the meaning of Pentecost.

PART 1

Five people stand in line. They look directly ahead and speak the lines naturally and sincerely. They must not sound like robots! They are not really aware of one another until the very end when the fifth person speaks for the final time.

A: I was at this wedding, right, and he turned the water into wine.
B: He raised a man from the dead.
C: I've seen him walk on the water!
D: He was in the temple casting out demons.
E: Jesus said that he would die.
A: He made a leper clean again.
B: I happen to know that he fed the entire crowd with five loaves and two fishes.
C: I saw him heal a man who had a withered hand.
D: There's no doubt about it – he's the greatest leader of all time.
E: He said he would die.

A: You know the blind man that used to beg in the temple courtyard? Well, he's not blind any more thanks to Jesus.

B: I've heard that he even healed a paralysed man and made him walk again.

C: He said that he'll save us . . . and he will!

D: He is truly a man without sin.

E: But he's going to die – for us.

PART II

Enter a REPORTER *and a group of people including* MARY *and* PETER. *The* REPORTER *moves from one to another in the group, stopping to interview each person. The rest of the group must react by showing great interest and generating the excitement of the occasion.*

REPORTER: Jerusalem. A city in confusion. After the death of the popular teacher, Jesus, many people sense that great loss that had been spoken about even before his crucifixion. Was he guilty of any crime? Did he have to die? What will happen now? Who knows?

I am standing near to a garden where there are reports of Jesus having been seen – alive. Here with me now is a witness to that event. Tell us, what did you see?

MARY: A gardener. Well at least that's who I thought it was at first, but there was something familiar about this man. I know who I wanted to see, who I longed to see, but this just seemed impossible. It was . . . it really was Jesus. He's alive!

(Reaction from group)

REPORTER: And you, sir, what is your name?

PETER: My name is Peter.

REPORTER: And did you know this man?

PETER: *(Boldly)* Yes. Yes I most certainly did. I've been frightened to say that before but now I'm not afraid any more. I'm going to tell everyone I know that Jesus has come back to life – just as he promised. He never breaks his promise. Everything he ever said was the truth and I am telling

you the truth now. He is alive and has returned
to us.

REPORTER: These are quite incredible scenes, ladies and
gentlemen. Jerusalem, our capital, is certainly a
city of amazing happenings. Surely nothing
else can surprise us now!

PART III

*The scene is similar to the previous one with a group of people
watching the proceedings.*

REPORTER: Jesus has returned to his Father. Jerusalem did
have further surprises after all. You, sir, what
can you tell us about the latest happening in the
story of Jesus?

MAN: He has gone to prepare a place for us. A place in
his Father's house, he says.

REPORTER: And you, madam, have you any evidence of
whether he will return again?

WOMAN: Yes. He will return, but no one knows how or
when. But, like all his promises, this will come
true some day.

REPORTER: And how will you cope now that he has left this
earth?

WOMAN: With difficulty of course. But he did say that he
would be sending a helper.

MAN: That's right, and we are going to wait for that
helper to arrive.

REPORTER: This helper . . . is it another teacher and healer?

WOMAN: No. That would be impossible. There can never
be another like Jesus.

REPORTER: But I suppose a whole army of people would be
needed to replace this great man?

MAN: It may be like that. We shall wait and see.

REPORTER: Won't you find the waiting rather tedious?

WOMAN: At times, perhaps. But patience will be
rewarded. You can be sure of that.

REPORTER: Thank you. Will patience be rewarded? What
will the helper be like? How long will we have
to wait? When we have the answers then you
will be the first to know.

(Group disperses)

Scraggle

Bible basis: Jesus heals a paralysed man
Matthew 9.1–8; Luke 5.17–26

Character: ARTHUR SCRAGGLE, a builder

Property: Telephone which rings at the start

The National Exhibition Centre in Birmingham has probably been the largest venue for the piece and it was beamed by satellite around the world. Quite what the churches in Korea made of it I would love to know!

The following script acts as a guideline to the performance, and the ending can be altered to suit the mood of the performer or audience.

There is a telephone ringing on stage. SCRAGGLE *enters. He is reasonably successful in his own business but does tend to sidetrack easily. The person phoning brings him back to reality with quite a bump each time.*

SCRAGGLE: Hello there . . . Scraggle here . . . that's right, Arthur Scraggle. Yeah – we do repairs to 'ouses. What's the problem? You've got a hole in your roof? . . . No sweat. Is it a big hole? Oh, that big. What caused that then? Dry rot? Rising damp? . . . Oh a bed came through the roof . . . so it's not the roof then but the ceiling . . . Oh it is the roof . . . the bed was on the roof then – been decorating have you? Had to make more room? . . . Oh some friends did it. Yes, there's been a lot of bother these days – riots and what have you – 'course it's the government I blame – they tread all over us little blokes . . . taxing this, taxing that . . . can't build here, can't build there. Here I am trying to do an honest day's work, well 9 to 5 that is . . . with an hour off for lunch and two coffee breaks in the morning . . . no we don't have coffee breaks in the afternoon, we prefer tea . . .

Now, where was I? Back door to be fixed was
it? . . . Oh no – the roof, that's right . . . yeah,
'course we'll fix it. Arthur Scraggle and brothers
– major repairs a speciality. No . . . Scraggle
. . . Arthur Scraggle . . . no that's the other one
. . . yes the names are similar . . . we do major
repairs . . . he deals with the minor ones . . .
So you say this hole was caused by your friends
shoving a bed . . . oh they didn't shove it . . .
they lowered it with someone on it . . . go on
. . . sort of joke was it? A bet, eh? . . . oh he was
sick . . . oh yes, sorry . . . didn't think of that.
You sure your door don't want fixing? Sounds a
bit barmy coming in through the roof . . . oh
the room was crowded. How is the bloke now?
Still sick, eh? You show me one person that gets
better on this Health Service . . . 'course there's
too many bosses and not enough doing the real
work. Now if they had a real union they'd . . .
what? He did what? Walked home? I thought
you said he was sick . . . who was he then? . . .
No don't know him . . . Where? . . . What that
chap that used to sit by the city gate? . . . Never
. . . go on . . . what, got up and walked? On
his own? . . . but that's a miracle! Who's his
doctor? . . . What do you mean, he ain't got a
doctor? You don't get fit by dropping through a
roof on a bed . . . I wish you did though – it
would be good for business. Jesus? He wasn't
in your house, was he? . . . really? . . . Yeah, I'll
bet it was crowded . . . I've heard he's a good
bloke . . . yeah . . . done a lot of good he has
. . . what union's he with? Scripture Union is
it? . . . Pardon? Telecom? . . . Oh, Holycom . . .
is that a union of hole fixers is it? . . . No, never
heard of it . . . Holy Comm-union . . . who's the
leader? . . . oh . . . oh him . . . sounds impress-
ive . . . what's the membership like? . . . Oh
good . . . still growing is it? And does this
Jesus always lead the meetings? . . . Really . . .

what, anyone can? I suppose they'd have to be
card holders, eh? . . . You just need two or three
gathered together? Is it true that he made a blind
man see? . . . It is? . . . Wow . . . and what
about these other miracles he's supposed to do?
. . . Are they true? What, all of them? Amazing
. . . he'd make a great speaker at our next union
meeting . . . oh has he? . . . Moved on . . . oh
. . . pity . . . I'd like to have met him. Can I?
When? Where? . . . Up on the Mount . . . yeah I
know it. What, a big open-air meeting? . . .
How long will it last? Should I bring something
to eat? I wouldn't mind betting he could provide the grub too . . . good that isn't it? That
would be a miracle! . . . Don't know what the
catering union would say though – that could
be a tricky one to deal with . . . you know . . .
own area and what have you . . . awkward for a
man in my position. Perhaps I'd better not come
. . well, all right, I'd better think about it but
. . . you know . . . own business . . . I've got
my brothers to consider. Yeah, I know that but I
can't commit myself too much. Look I'll just
come and fix your roof in the morning and we'll
chat more then . . . OK? . . . A quote? . . . Well,
it's not easy . . . look . . . if you don't say anything to your neighbours I'll do it . . . well . . .
cost price . . . perhaps a bit less, you know, for
him. Well no, I meant the sick bloke . . . not him
. . . but I suppose I'll do it for him too. But don't
spread it around – it'd be bad for business. I
don't want people to see Scraggle as a softie.
Sorry about the roof . . . and your friend . . .
no, I suppose I wouldn't have spoken to you
otherwise . . . no I don't talk about . . . you
know . . . God and Jesus much . . . should I?
Yeah, well I'll be round in the morning . . . yeah
that's what I'll do – I'll be round in the morning.
Cheers. *(He starts to put the phone down.)* Wow! I
don't believe it . . . I've just offered to do a job

for less than cost price. That's not like me . . .
what's come over me then? I heard something
about Jesus changing people's lives . . . but I
never thought he'd bother with me! *(He replaces
the phone and – if appropriate – exits, calling)* 'Ere,
Joan, guess what's happened . . . I've just been
talking about Jesus . . .

Going back

Bible basis: Return and reconciliation
Philemon

Characters: NARRATOR
PHILEMON
ONESIMUS
RICH
DRUNK
BEAUTY
PAUL

Scene: An area with three doors

Properties: Money
Bottle and glasses
Party streamers
Pen and paper

The Bible is full of interesting "ordinary" characters and so the idea of dramatizing one such person appealed.

The three main characters, PHILEMON, ONESIMUS *and* PAUL *are talking together in front of the doors. They are sharing some joke or other and do not notice that the sketch has begun.*

NARRATOR: We now present a story of three characters who had never all met each other although each knew of the others' existence.
(The three at their doors sneak behind hoping nobody has noticed them! The NARRATOR *comes forward.)*

NARRATOR: In the early Church, at a time when slavery was common, and generally accepted by most religions, new converts found it hard to understand the relationship that should exist between slave and master. This is an example of one such problem which we read about in a small book of the Bible.
(Goes to PHILEMON's *"door" and knocks loudly.)*

PHILEMON: *(Angrily)* What do you think you are doing?

typical of your sort. I hope you'll offer me a new tin of paint to cover up the damage you've caused.

NARRATOR: Well, I . . .

PHILEMON: You can't fool me so don't try and gloss over the facts. *(He goes behind the door again.)*

NARRATOR: That was Mr Phil Lemon who . . .

PHILEMON: Philemon *(Pronounced Fy-Lee-Mon.)*

NARRATOR: Sorry . . . Philemon. A hard task master and not exactly everyone's favourite boss. His slave is called Onesimus (ONESIMUS *appears*) and he, naturally, lives at Phil Lemon's house.

ONESIMUS: Don't let him hear you call him that! He'll turn very nasty.

NARRATOR: And is that a nasty sight?

ONESIMUS: You'd better believe it. He gives me a dog's life.

NARRATOR: What! Just because you might call him Phil Lemon by mistake?

PHILEMON: *(Entering)* Onesimus . . . walkies! (ONESIMUS *obeys with a shrug to the* NARRATOR*)* Good boy. Sit! Roll over. (ONESIMUS *does all these things*) Die for your country. There's a good boy. Now . . . don't let me hear that name again. *(He exits.)*

NARRATOR: I see what you mean. So you don't like working for him then?

ONESIMUS: No way. And he's supposed to be a Christian. Well if that's Christianity then I'm off. *(He leaves.)*

NARRATOR: And that is precisely what he did . . . upped and left right down the road.
(ONESIMUS tries to work out these directions.)
I said he upped and left right down the road.

ONESIMUS: Did you say left or right?

NARRATOR: I said you left. Right?

ONESIMUS: Right.

NARRATOR: Left!

ONESIMUS: Oh I left. Right!

PHILEMON: Wrong.

ONESIMUS: Right! I left. *(He finally goes from sight.)*

NARRATOR: This did not please Philemon.

PHILEMON: *(Coming forward)* I am not pleased.

NARRATOR: Where could he find another slave like Onesimus? *(PHILEMON circles the NARRATOR, eyeing him/her up and down)* Who would work for the likes of him? *(Noticing PHILEMON)* Surely nobody would. Nobody . . . no . . . no . . . no!!

PHILEMON: *(Gleefully nodding)* Sit. *(NARRATOR obeys)* Roll over. Die for your country. Walkies . . . *(They begin to leave.)*

NARRATOR: But I'm only meant to be narrating this sketch.

PHILEMON: Well now you've got the lead!

(ONESIMUS comes forward when the way is clear.)

ONESIMUS: I'm free! Free to go where I want . . . free to do what I want. Fantastic, *(Pause)* yes . . . great. *(Longer pause)* Free. *(Even longer pause)* Where shall I go? I know. I'll go over there. No I won't. I'll go that way. Or perhaps over here. You see I'm free to choose. I can go any way that I want. *(He pauses)* I think I'll stay here. *(He stands very still for a while.)*

(Enter RICH, a person with plenty of money. He stops near ONESIMUS and counts it out – tempting him to follow.)

RICH: My boy, money makes the world go round. Without it you're a nobody. I could use a bright lad like you – I'd make you rich beyond your wildest dreams. Follow me to the Rolls!

(RICH starts to leave and ONESIMUS begins following but is distracted by the entry of a DRUNK festooned in party streamers, carrying a bottle and glasses. ONESIMUS remains to watch.)

DRUNK: Feeling down, lad? Come and have a drink or three . . . it'll make you feel much better. I can show you a good time. Follow me – the bar's this way.

(DRUNK leaves alone. BEAUTY appears behind ONESIMUS and tries to tempt him to follow. She very nearly succeeds.)

BEAUTY: Come up and see me some time!

(BEAUTY *exits alone. Enter* PAUL)

PAUL: Jesus said "Follow me".

ONESIMUS: Pardon?

PAUL: Jesus said "Follow me".

ONESIMUS: Oh . . . I see. *(He looks sideways at* PAUL. PAUL *nods encouragingly.)* Follow (PAUL *nods again*) . . . follow me. Right – I get it – Jesus said "Follow me".

PAUL: So?

ONESIMUS: So I follow you. Right?

PAUL: No. You follow Jesus.

ONESIMUS: Oh you're not Jesus then?

PAUL: No. My name is Paul and I am one of his followers. It is Jesus Christ you must follow.

ONESIMUS: I've heard that before somewhere . . . back at my master's house I think it was.

PAUL: Who is that?

ONESIMUS: *(Not thinking)* Philemon.

PAUL: Did you say Philemon?

ONESIMUS: *(Warily, having blundered)* Well some people call him that but I . . .

PAUL: He's a good friend of mine. How is he? I haven't seen him for ages and ages. I've been in prison you know.

ONESIMUS: *(Aside)* Just my luck! A friend of Philemon who'll probably murder me. *(To* PAUL*)* Did you say prison?

PAUL: Yes.

ONESIMUS: *(Smiles)* Great. *(Drops smile)* Goodbye. *(He starts to leave.)*

PAUL: Yes – I'm afraid so. That was for following Jesus.

ONESIMUS: You went to prison?

PAUL: Yes.

ONESIMUS: For following Jesus?

(Freeze. The NARRATOR *steps forward.)*

NARRATOR: Paul then told Onesimus about the gospel of Jesus. They met and prayed together a lot and Onesimus decided to follow Jesus. He became a Christian. At a later meeting, Onesimus said to Paul . . .

ONESIMUS: Paul, I want to return to Philemon and apologize for running away. I must forgive him for the way he treated me and ask for his forgiveness too.

PAUL: Good. I'll write a letter for you to take.

(PAUL *goes to the pen and paper and starts to write. Lines are occasionally heard.*)

PAUL: To Philemon, our dear friend and fellow worker . . . every time I pray, I mention you and give thanks to my God, because I hear of your faith in the Lord Jesus. I am making a request to you on behalf of Onesimus . . . I am sending him back to you . . . perhaps the reason he was separated from you for a while is that you might have him back not as a slave but as a dear Christian brother . . . if he has done you any wrong or owes you anything charge it to me . . . Please get a room ready for me as I hope to see you soon . . . The grace of the Lord Jesus be with your spirit . . .

(PAUL *gives the letter to* ONESIMUS *who begins to leave.*)

ONESIMUS: Look at that! I'm going down in history! I'm only a little part . . . but I'm there.

Garments

Bible basis: Clothes
Genesis 37; Luke 23.11–12, 8.43–48

Characters: Three narrators: ONE, TWO & THREE
CROWD, doubling as
JESUS
WOMAN
JOSEPH
JOSEPH'S BROTHERS

Properties: Large brightly coloured length of material
Bible

Experiment with the material, and see how soft, gentle, strong, tight it can be made just by holding it in different ways.

Consider a crowd of people. A crowd who welcomed Jesus into Jerusalem. "Hosanna" they cried and waved their branches in the air. A short time later that same crowd called for him to be put to death. "Crucify him" was their cry.

Garments tries to reflect some of those changes that occur in individuals and groups and the piece of material is the way of showing these changes. It is probably easiest to get three people to read it aloud while the others do battle with the cloth! It is an important member of the cast, and it can also be used for a few comic effects but these must be very carefully handled so as not to ruin any serious messages that might be presented. The cast need to act all the time to help the narrators with the sketch. It needs to be fast-moving and has to create rapid changes of mood. It has the speed of a quick change artist!

The cast are behind a cloak or piece of material that acts as a curtain. It is wrapped around them all at the start but becomes the clothing of just a central figure at the appropriate moment.

ONE: This is the story of . . .
TWO: Clothes for hire!
THREE: Clothes for hire!
ONE: What?
TWO: Clothes for hire.

THREE: Clothes for hire.

ONE: Are you sure?

TWO: Yes, we're sure.

THREE: Yes, we're sure.

ONE: Could I ask something?

TWO: Of course.

THREE: Of course.

ONE: Why do you repeat everything?

TWO: Do we?

THREE: Do we?

ONE: Yes, you do.

TWO: I'm sure you're right.

THREE: I'm sure you're right.

ONE: Then that makes you . . .

TWO ⎫
THREE ⎭ Doubly sure!

(They wait for response from audience. Nothing.)

ONE: *(Unperturbed)* This is the story of clothes.

TWO: Clothes for hire!

THREE: Ah! Thank you. I'll have some.

ONE: This is the High Priest.

TWO: *(Questioning)* Yes . . . ?

THREE: And it says here *(Points to Bible)*

TWO: Yes . . . ?

THREE: It says here that the High Priest rent his clothes.

ONE: Oh boy. This is dreadful.

TWO: Were they dear?

THREE: Yes.

ONE: What a rip off!

(A crowd of people press around the figure of JESUS *who is seen wearing the cloak. When the* WOMAN *touches the cloak it must be held in such a way that the audience (and cast) are aware that something has happened.)*

TWO: And a great throng were around Jesus as he passed . . .

THREE: And a woman

ONE: Who had been bleeding for many years

TWO: Reached out

THREE: And touched

ONE: His cloak

TWO: And was cured

THREE: By her faith.

(The WOMAN *leaves the scene keeping her eyes on the cloak. She rejoins the cast. The cast is again behind the cloak.)*

ONE: Joseph's brothers were jealous.

(The jealous BROTHERS *peer out from behind the cloak which is now being worn by* JOSEPH. *Get some laughs here with the jealous faces!)*

Joseph's brothers were jealous

TWO: When Jacob bought his son a coat

THREE: Of many colours.

ONE: It was red

TWO: And yellow

THREE: And green

ONE: And blue

TWO: And orange

THREE: And pink

ONE: And red

TWO: And yellow

THREE: And red

ONE: And yellow

TWO: And red

THREE: And . . . um . . . yellow

ONE: And lots of nice shades

TWO: And tints

THREE: And hues

ONE: Whose?

TWO: Hugh's

THREE: Who's Hugh?

ONE: Hues . . . shades . . .

TWO: Sunglasses?

CAST: No!

ONE: Well . . . Jacob's sons were green with envy

TWO: Jacob's sons were red with rage

THREE: Jacob's sons were cream with crackers!

ONE: But Joseph was strong

TWO: He was protected

THREE: From death

ONE: From trials

TWO: From tribulations.

THREE: He was protected from . . .

ONE: Enemies

TWO: From adversity

THREE: And from the rain (CAST *act sheltering from rain*)

ONE: *(Firmly)* Of Pharoah.

TWO: He was protected

THREE: As if by a guardian angel.

ONE: St Michael.

TWO: Why St Michael?

ONE: He's a cardigan angel.

TWO: *(Looks a bit sheepish)* Baa! Baa!

THREE: What are you up to?

TWO: It says here that I should look a bit sheepish.

(A slight pause as the mood changes. The cloak is now billowed in front of JESUS *as the* CROWD *line the route. The movement of the material must be soft and gentle to contrast with the harsh appearance of the material at the moment of crucifixion.)*

ONE: And as he entered Jerusalem upon a colt

TWO: The people threw down their cloaks

THREE: And strew palm leaves in his way

(The cloak is rolled up tightly as the next few pieces are enacted.)

ONE: And they took him into the courtyard

TWO: And whipped

THREE: And stripped him.

ONE: The soldiers spat on him

THREE: Then draped a purple cloak about him.

ONE: A crown of thorns was placed upon his head

TWO: And they led him away

(The tight roll of cloth is placed behind JESUS *and is used to lead him away.)*

THREE: To be crucified.

(The cloth is pulled tight and JESUS *hangs upon it. Silence. The cloth is used to lower* JESUS *to the ground. It is then unrolled to form a screen which falls over the body as the narration starts.)*

ONE: But the stone was rolled away

TWO: And there in the darkness of the cave
THREE: Lay the clothes that had adorned our Lord
ONE: He had risen
TWO: As he said he would.
(An actor lifts the material making it resemble a baby wrapped in sheets.)
THREE: The babe from Bethlehem
ONE: Wrapped in swaddling clothes
TWO: Has risen
THREE: And sits as a king
ONE: The King of kings
TWO: Dressed in bright raiment
THREE: At the side of his Father.
(The cast form around a central figure – a "baby".)
ONE: We are now his body on earth
TWO: And our lives are his garments.
THREE: They may mock
ONE: They may scorn
TWO: And our faith becomes torn
THREE: But our Lord gives us armour bright.
ONE: For his Church now is shown
TWO: In the talents we own
THREE: We are clothed
ONE: In his glorious light.

Perfect timing

Bible basis: The crossing of the Red Sea
Exodus 14.21–29

Characters: SHOPPER
NEIGHBOUR
WORKER
JIM
GIRLFRIEND
BOYFRIEND
FATHER (MR ELIOT)

Scene: Bus stop

Properties: Bags of shopping
Newspapers

The parting of the Red Sea, which forms a basis of the sketch,
may not happen to us in our lives but the perfect timing of God
is very real.

As the sketch is set at a bus stop it should not take an
enormous leap of imagination to see how this could be used
out of doors! It would work well in any setting.

*A bus has just left. (A sound effect could be used.) Assorted people
rush in laden with shopping, etc. and express their dismay at having
missed the bus.* JIM *is among them. They are not strangers to one
another – perhaps neighbours or workmates?*

SHOPPER:	On no! My feet are killing me.
NEIGHBOUR:	My mate's going to kill me if I'm late.
WORKER:	Since when has the bus left at this time?
SHOPPER:	I shall have to sit down.
NEIGHBOUR:	She'll never believe I missed the bus.
WORKER:	It's one hold up after another these days.
JIM:	There'll be another one again soon.
SHOPPER:	Oh yes . . . that's easy to say. What about my feet?
NEIGHBOUR:	And what about my mate?
WORKER:	At least I'll have time to read the paper. I can't abide reading on a bus.

JIM: The wait will give us a chance to get our breath back.

(They all become resigned to their wait and line up at the bus stop. The WORKER *reads a paper, others read, look around, check shopping, etc.)*

JIM: *(To* WORKER*)* Anything happened in the world today?

WORKER: No. Same old stories of doom and gloom.

SHOPPER: Why can't they print good news for a change?

NEIGHBOUR: My friend says good news doesn't sell papers.

JIM: How come the Bible's always been a best seller then?

SHOPPER: Ooh yes . . . they call it the Good News Bible don't they?

NEIGBOUR: Is it really a best seller?

WORKER: That's right: the world's best seller. There's more Bibles in people's homes than any other book.

SHOPPER: Funny thing that.

WORKER: What?

SHOPPER: Well. I was just thinking . . . it's the book that's bought the most yet the one that's read the least.

NEIGHBOUR: Who says?

SHOPPER: Well. I don't know for sure of course. But I'll bet we've all got Bibles, but how many of us read them?

JIM: I do.

WORKER: Not enough time.

NEIGHBOUR: Don't understand all the long words.

SHOPPER: Shame that.

(They go back to their reading etc. The SHOPPER *still thinks about the conversation. The* WORKER *and the* NEIGHBOUR *appear to forget it.* JIM *looks around the street, looks at watch, etc. He observes two people coming. They are a* BOYFRIEND *and* GIRLFRIEND *and they join the queue slightly apart from the others.)*

BOYFRIEND: Looks like we missed the bus, love.

GIRLFRIEND: What a pain! Must be a new timetable or something.

BOYFRIEND: More likely their timing's up the shoot again.
(They do not take part in the conversation of the others, but are listening all the same.)

WORKER: *(Looking in paper)* I see the weather's playing up again.

JIM: How's that?

WORKER: Floods, freak tides. Just listen to this: "Freak weather conditions have again resulted in some unexpected happenings around the coast. Off the Cayman Islands it was reported that local fishermen actually saw the sea part in two."

SHOPPER: Did it really? Crumbs, I thought that only happened in Moses' time.

WORKER: No, it says that it's happened on a number of occasions.

NEIGHBOUR: Wasn't Moses special then?

JIM: Yes. He led his people to the promised land.

SHOPPER: All those that were following got swallowed up in the sea when it went back together.

NEIGHBOUR: Was it just a tidal wave then?

WORKER: 'Course it was. Hardly a miracle . . . happens all the time.

JIM: Timing was good though.

WORKER: Eh?

JIM: Well if it happens all the time, which I think is an exaggeration, it was clever timing for Moses and his people to be standing just at the right place for them to cross over. What do you think?

WORKER: Well . . . yes . . . I suppose so . . .

SHOPPER: Brilliant timing if you ask me.

JIM: God's chosen people were saved by him intervening. Perfect timing. If the sea hadn't parted at Moses' command, then who knows where we'd be now.

SHOPPER: Not stood waiting for a bus. That's for sure.
(They consider this conversation for a while. They cannot help but overhear the next conversation but take no active part in it.)

BOYFRIEND: So what do you reckon then?

GIRLFRIEND: About what?

BOYFRIEND: What I said earlier. You know . . . this weekend. My folks are going away for a few days. We'd have the place to ourselves.

GIRLFRIEND: I don't think we should.

BOYFRIEND: Where's the harm in it?

GIRLFRIEND: Well . . . you know . . .

BOYFRIEND: But you love me don't you?

GIRLFRIEND: Of course I do. But it wouldn't be right to stay the weekend with you.

BOYFRIEND: Don't see why not.

(MR ELIOT *joins the queue as the following exchange is made.*)

GIRLFRIEND: I don't think we should spend the weekend together that's all.

BOYFRIEND: But nothing would happen.

ELIOT: Too right nothing's going to happen!

GIRLFRIEND: Dad!

BOYFRIEND: Mr Eliot!

ELIOT: Yes – Mr Eliot – and what, may I ask, were you two planning?

BOYFRIEND: Well . . . it's . . .

GIRLFRIEND: Dad . . . it's like this . . .

ELIOT: (*Aware that everyone is now listening*) I don't think this is the time or the place to discuss this matter. Do you?

BOYFRIEND: No, Mr Eliot. But I can explain . . .

GIRLFRIEND: We didn't expect to see you at this time, Dad.

ELIOT: Apparently not. I got a lift to the school expecting to meet you as you came out. Just as well I did I think.

GIRLFRIEND: You're right, Dad.

BOYFRIEND: Look, I think I'll walk home. I'll be seeing you sometime. OK?

GIRLFRIEND: OK. 'Bye.

(BOYFRIEND *leaves hurriedly.*)

ELIOT: It might be an idea if we walked for a while as well. Perhaps we can chat on the way.

(MR ELIOT *and* GIRLFRIEND *leave too. The relationship between them seems good.*)

SHOPPER: (*To* WORKER *and* JIM) Bit of bad luck for those two schemers, eh?

WORKER: If the bus had been on time they would have had their weekend together.

JIM: Rather like a present-day Moses scene.

WORKER: How do you mean?

JIM: The father intervened. I'm telling you . . . God's timing is always perfect.

NEIGHBOUR: Look, the bus has stopped down there. Come on or we'll miss it. *(He rushes off.)*

(They move off in the same direction as the NEIGHBOUR. JIM *helps the* SHOPPER *with her bags. The* WORKER *folds his paper and leaves thoughtfully, intending to talk more on the bus.)*

A pair of trainers

Bible basis: Preparing for evangelism
Acts 4; Colossians 4.2

Characters: DES IRVING
ALBERT ROSS

Properties: Envelope containing a letter
Coloured leaflets
Booklets
Manuals

We have probably all seen examples of good and bad training
– in whatever field. Here is a fast-moving sketch that shows
how not to do it and, as a result, shows the right way to begin
such training. There is no reason why the characters have to be
men – I just liked their names!

An envelope arrives on stage as if delivered through a letter box. DES
and ALBERT *rush in and grapple for the envelope. It is* DES *who
succeeds in opening it.*

DES: It's come. This is it!

ALBERT: Well come on then, read it out. Let's get started.

DES: "To Mr Des Irving and Mr Albert Ross. Here, as
requested, is your step-by-step guide to street
evangelism. With this handy booklet you can
expect to witness to people at any time and in
any place."

ALBERT: Sounds just the thing!

DES: "Thousands of people have used this course
and are now confident in their street evangelism. Go on, try it. Turn over."

ALBERT: Eh?

DES: Turn over! Oh . . . I'm at the bottom of the page.
We don't have to turn over! Look, there's more
on the back.
*(He turns the letter and dozens of coloured leaflets
flutter to the ground.* ALBERT *picks them up
untidily.)*

"Go on. Try it and see but remember that the
first thing you should always do . . ."

ALBERT: I hope these weren't in any special order!

DES: *(Putting down letter and picking up leaflet)* Oh, it
won't matter, surely. Look, this one's got a
number one on it. "Training manual" it says.
(He opens it) "Welcome to your step by step
guide to blah . . . blah . . . now that you have
finished . . . blah blah" *(He turns pages quickly)*
ah . . . this is where it starts . . . never mind all
that waffle at the beginning.

ALBERT: Are you sure? We might have missed something important!

DES: Nonsense! I know all about these courses.
There's no need to read the introductions. Get
straight to the action I say. Do you know,
Albert, by lunch time we could be in the pre-
cinct stopping people and converting them on
the spot. What a challenge, eh?

ALBERT: How do we begin?

DES: *(Turning to manual page and reading)* "For this
lesson you need a partner." *(To ALBERT)* That will
have to be you. *(Reading again)* "Get your
partner to hold the leaflets for you until you feel
confident enough to put away this manual. The
instructions are very simple. Don't worry if you
get things wrong first time, but remember – in
the street you may have only one chance to talk
to a stranger about the Lord." Albert, this is
fantastic. What an opportunity.

ALBERT: Fire away, Des. I've got all the blurb. Let's give
it a whirl!

DES: *(Reading on)* It says to try and make the meeting
as natural as possible. Get your partner to
pretend to be in the street as you approach.

ALBERT: Got it. Here goes. *(Shouting)* Papers! Papers!
Read all about it!

DES: *(Shouting above it)* Excuse me . . .

ALBERT: Echo! Echo! Judges to act on indecent shows!

DES: Albert!

ALBERT: Soccer spe . . . *(Normally)* sorry?

DES: Could we have a little less of the rhetoric?

ALBERT: But I thought it would be good if I was someone in the street . . . like a news vendor.

DES: Couldn't you just be walking along as I approach?

ALBERT: Fine. I'll start over here.

(DES and ALBERT now move as far apart as possible, turn and stroll towards one another. As ALBERT is close to DES, DES puts out an arm. ALBERT collides with the arm and is winded.)

DES: Sorry, mate. I thought it would be good if I extended a hand of friendship.

ALBERT: *(Still winded)* Where does it say you have to attack people before converting them?

DES: I said I'm sorry. Look, go back and try again.

(They both retreat and try again. ALBERT keeps a very wary eye on DES this time as they approach one another.)

DES: What are you doing?

ALBERT: I'm approaching you like you said.

DES: But we're supposed to be strangers. Why are you looking at me like that?

ALBERT: I don't want to be hurt again!

DES: All right, let's suppose we've met at last. *(Reads)* "Good morning. My name is Insert."

ALBERT: Des! Insert your own name there.

DES: "My name is Des. Are you in a hurry?"

ALBERT: Yes. *(He goes away.)*

DES: Oi! You're supposed to say no. It says so here in the manual.

ALBERT: But what if the person is in a hurry?

DES: How should I know? *(Reads again)* Oh here it is. "If the person says yes, then say immediately 'I've got some good news for you.'"

ALBERT: That's clever. Yes! No one would walk away from that!

DES: ". . . good news that will change your life. Look at this booklet with me."

(ALBERT takes the first booklet and reads the title.)

ALBERT: "A death in the family"

DES: What?

ALBERT: "A death in the family"

DES: The red booklet . . . not the black one!

ALBERT: Well you didn't tell me! How was I to know? They're all muddled up I expect. *(Finds red booklet)* "Good news to you."

DES: *(Turning page of manual)* "I'm going to read this booklet with you and ask you some questions. OK?"

(ALBERT is absorbed in the booklet and turns the pages over hurriedly.)

DES: I said "OK?" Are you listening to me or not?

ALBERT: Sorry. I was reading this.

DES: Well you mustn't.

ALBERT: But you just said we were going to read it so I'm reading it. You can't keep changing your mind, you know. Either we are going to read it or we're not going to read it. There's no two ways about it, you know. If you don't want to read it then that's fine by me but I'm going to read it. It was your idea in the first place and now I'm just taking your idea and I'm going to read it. When I've finished reading it then it'll be your turn or else we could share and read it together. I don't mind. But read it you said, and read it I will. So there.

DES: Finished?

ALBERT: Reading?

DES: No! Talking! We are supposed to be practising this evangelism in the peace and tranquillity of our own home and all you succeed in doing is messing it up.

ALBERT: Me mess it up? Well I like that! Who was it knocked me for six? Who gave me the books in the wrong order? Who won't let me read in peace? Good news? This is the worst news I've ever had in my life.

(He throws all the booklets except one in the air, stomps across to a chair and sits with his back to DES.)

ALBERT: Hmph!

DES: Where's that letter? *(He searches through all the debris and finally retrieves it.)* Here it is. "Go on. Try it, but remember the first thing you should always do is pray. *(He is subdued as he reads this and* ALBERT *half turns to listen as he proceeds.)* Pray for an opportunity. Pray for the right words at the right time. Pray for the person you are about to meet. The whole exercise of street witness has to be surrounded by prayer. Now before you start, take time to pray over the booklet. To rush this activity spells failure. To go out in the street without prayer would be a recipe for disaster.

ALBERT: *(Looking at the booklet he kept)* "Before Jesus faced the agony of the cross he prayed. By prayer, you can receive the Holy Spirit and with this power you can move mountains.

DES: Albert?

ALBERT: You don't have to say anything mate.

DES: I think it's about time we prayed. Yes?

ALBERT: Too right!

Sam

Bible basis: The Good Samaritan and forgiveness
Luke 10.25–37; Matthew 18.21–35

Character: SAM, a small boy
Scene: A room with either a telephone or a bed

Sam is based on one of the best known parables, The Good Samaritan, and the audience will probably know the story well enough to appreciate all the references made within the sketch. If they don't, then you could always read the story beforehand!

However, this is not the story of the Good Samaritan in dramatic form. Rather this is a conversation between a boy (Sam) and God. Many people cannot believe that God is everywhere or that he listens to every prayer that is given up in his name. Such are the thoughts of Sam as he talks to God. He is a little boy and he could either be talking to God by telephone or kneeling at the foot of a bed. Like all good pray-ers, Sam leaves time for God to answer.

SAM *dials a number and waits for a reply, or he kneels at the foot of the bed with his hands together*

SAM: Hello! It's me . . . that's right . . . me. How did you know who it was? . . . Did you? . . . Did you? . . . Did you? . . . Wow, that's amazing . . . you actually knew it was me just when I said "Hello. It's me"? That's fantastic. Did you know it was me before I said it was me? . . . Did you? . . . Did you? . . . Did you?! Fancy that. I wish I could do that! It would be useful at school knowing the prefects were coming before they came . . . yeah . . . useful that . . .

Anyway, God, the reason I'm talking to you is that my mum and me have been having an argument about the ditch round the back . . . yeah, that's right . . . the ditch . . . yeah, that one

by the road. Well my mum says that me and my
mate Johnny can't play in the ditch 'cos there
might be thieves there or something and I said
"Don't be stupid, mum, the thieves would have
gone back to Jericho by now with all the man's
money" and she said don't call me stupid and
anyway God would have punished the thieves
by now and I said that they must have gone or
they would have attacked the Samaritan when
he helped the man what had got set on by
thieves and therefore it would be fine for me
and Johnny to go playing in the ditch and my
mum hit me.

So who's right? *(Sam crosses his fingers)* . . . But
I thought the ditch would be safe by now . . . yes
I know I should honour my mum and dad but
can't I play in the ditch? You'd protect me
wouldn't you? . . . and my mate Johnny? . . . 'cos
you protected the bloke what got set on and you
sent a helper . . . a sort of angel that Samaritan
was I reckon . . . and I bet you got rid of those
thieves too . . . what did you do? Zap them with
a lightning bolt? Flood them with a huge wave?
Send a cloud of grasshoppers to munch them
up? Go on . . . what did you do? . . . I know – you
got the whole Roman army to drive their
chariots all over them . . . yes? . . . and I'll bet
you squashed and stoned that rotten Levi . . .
I've heard of stone-squashed Levis before . . .
and what about that pathetic priest what
passed by on the other side? Did you kill him
too? Passed by, then passed on sort of thing?

Yes? . . . No? . . . No! . . . you forgave . . . you
forgave them? . . . What all of them? . . . and I've
got to forgive mum for smacking me? Well, just
this once then . . . no, I know, you told me before
. . . lots of times . . . *(Puzzled)* so would she
forgive me if I went in the ditch? . . . No . . . I
suppose not . . . how many times have I got to
forgive people? . . . how many? . . . seventy

times seven? But that's *(He does some complicated mental maths.)* . . . well it's . . . forty . . . forty thousand . . . well forty days and forty nights that means a lot doesn't it? . . . so I've got to forgive all those times then . . . OK . . . if you say so, God . . . and thanks . . . thanks for all them parables. They really make you think don't they?

Can I ask you just one more thing? . . . well it's this – why have mum and dad got to be like me? . . . no I don't mean looks . . . I mean like me . . . like children . . . oh I see . . . they've got to ask . . . like us children are always asking? I'll tell them . . . 'cos anyone can ask . . . you know, God, you really do make some things ever so easy . . . I mean . . . asking! *(He chuckles.)*

(To audience) Anyone can ask God for help . . . he's always got time for us and he forgives us all the time . . . well I'd better go and see what Johnny's up to . . . his mum's going shopping with my mum this afternoon so you know where he and I are going to play while they're not watching . . . yeah . . . we're going to play in the park. *(He exits, whistling.)*

Blinder

Bible basis: The third Commandment
Deuteronomy 5

Characters: DEREK, an odd-job man
PHIL, a would-be businessman
Scene: A room with a chair
Properties: Financial Times
Booklet

If you have two members in your group who work particularly well together, then use them in *Blinder*. Its success depends very much on the rapport between Derek and Phil and the audience has to warm to these two and laugh with them and at them.

DEREK *is sitting reading the Financial Times when* PHIL *enters from the hallway.* PHIL *is very thoughtful.* DEREK *glances at him but does not really listen to the start of the conversation.*

DEREK: Don't tell me . . . double glazing.
PHIL: No.
DEREK: Why do they use our patch as a training ground?
PHIL: No, it weren't the double glazing.
DEREK: Well, it wasn't the Avon lady, that's for sure. You weren't gone long enough.
PHIL: No. It was a bloke from some church or other. He gave me this little book.
(DEREK glances towards the booklet that PHIL holds.)
DEREK: Oh blimey, Phil, leave it off. I hope you told him where to go.
PHIL: Well . . . sort of . . .
DEREK: What do you mean? Sort of? I've got no time for these doorstep wallies. Bloomin' chatter day saints and witnesses for the persecution. Someone ought to invent a welcome mat with "clear off" printed on it.

PHIL: Don't be like that. This bloke was very interesting.

DEREK: Godswallop!

PHIL: Ha, ha . . . very funny. What do you know about it anyway?

DEREK: Look, Phil, you are talking to one of the converted.

PHIL: Get off, Derek . . . you ain't religious.

DEREK: I beg your pardon, but I've always been C. of E.

PHIL: What? Customs and Excise?

DEREK: Leave off! Christened and married in the C. of E. I was . . .Church of England born and bred . . . none of this doorstep rubbish.

PHIL: Well you know what they say: hatched, matched then despatched.

DEREK: Eh?

PHIL: Christened, wedded then deaded!

DEREK: Phil! Stop that talk. You know it's not the done thing to talk about dying. Anyway, it upsets 'er indoors. When I have to go and meet the Maker then I shall go.

PHIL: 'Course you'll go . . . there's no refusing, you know.

DEREK: I know that . . . 'course I know that . . . I just don't like talking about it. No, don't you worry, when it comes to my turn to join the angels then I shall be only too ready to play my harp.

PHIL: Makes a change from always being on the fiddle!

DEREK: Oh, very good. Look, I'm an honest businessman. I have nothing to hide.

PHIL: *(Looking at booklet)* You're different then . . . 'cos it says here that "everyone has sinned and is far away from God's saving presence. Romans 3.23."

DEREK: Look . . . I'm telling you . . . I have nothing to be ashamed of.

PHIL: That bloke from church – the one who gave me this – he was right, you know.

DEREK: *(Interested, despite himself)* What did he say then?

PHIL: *(Secretly looking into the book for his prompt)* Well, he said that God sees into the darkest corners of our lives.

DEREK: Nothing new there, my son. Is that all he had to say?

PHIL: He asked about the second coming.

DEREK: What, coming to church, you mean?

PHIL: Don't be daft!

DEREK: Well I go to church regular. Christmas, Easter, Harvest. Well 'er indoors likes to sing the carols and what have you. She likes the flowers too . . . not me . . . hay fever, you know.

PHIL: That ain't what he meant, Derek. He meant the second coming.

DEREK: Whose?

PHIL: Jesus'.

DEREK: Oh, blimey, Phil . . . you've been conned. How much did he rush you for?

PHIL: Nothing.

DEREK: Oh yeah? He'll be back rattling a tin under your nose. Some creaky spire got the beetle I expect . . . dry rot in the pulpit . . . they're always after something.

DEREK: Look if you want to know anything about Jesus you could ask me for free.

PHIL: You don't know the next thing about him.

DEREK: Cor blimey, Phil, you are only talking to the man who, as a boy, won the prize three years running at Sunday School.

PHIL: What for?

DEREK: For reciting Scripture, that's what.

PHIL: Well . . . go on then . . .

DEREK: Go on what?

PHIL: Recite something.

DEREK: *(Waffling)* You think I can't, don't you? Well you are wrong.

PHIL: Go on then, cleverclogs. Prove it.

DEREK: I'm thinking. Jesus wept, why has everything got to be such a rush?

PHIL: Was that it?

DEREK: Was what it?

PHIL: "Jesus wept." Is that your prize winning verse?

DEREK: *(At first unaware that he has quoted)* What? No . . .
oh I see . . . there . . . that just proves how
natural it is for me to talk religious.

PHIL: Come on. You never talk religious.

DEREK: You know nothing. I have a great respect for our
Lord.

PHIL: Why say "Jesus wept", then?

DEREK: Well . . .

PHIL: Look Derek, next time that bloke calls we'll talk
to him.

DEREK: Not on your nelly! You won't get me
chinwagging with some Holy Joe! They're only
after your money.

PHIL: You have got to be joking. This is not a game you
know.

DEREK: Of course it is. Life is a game of billiards . . .

BOTH: Till someone snookers it up.

DEREK: Oh . . . you heard it before?

PHIL: Talking about Jesus isn't a game according to
that bloke.

DEREK: Look . . . clear off, will you? You're like some
good Samaritan trying to get me out of the
ditch.

PHIL: Well that's where the thieves were!

DEREK: Oi! Push off and get that van unloaded.

PHIL: All right . . . I'm going . . . and I'll unload the
van . . . and I'll be thinking about it all.
*(He happens to throw the book down within DEREK'S
reach. DEREK notices this but makes no move yet.)*
I'll see you then. And remember . . .

DEREK: What?

PHIL: Don't take his name in vain, OK?
(He exits.)

DEREK: *(Returning to paper)* Bloomin' freaks knocking
on the door. Cor blimey, what do they think
they're playing at? What's it got to do with me?
*(He makes sure PHIL isn't looking as he picks up the
book and begins to read.)*

Well *(Turns page)* . . . yeah . . . that could be me
. . . perhaps there is something in this religion
after all.
*(PHIL has returned, unbeknown to DEREK, and stops
behind him and grins.)*

I stand at the door

Bible basis: Jesus says "Come to me"
Matthew 11.28; Luke 11.9–13; Revelation 3.20

Characters: VICAR
                 LADY (MRS FROBISHER)
                 GIRL
                 OLD MAN
                 MAJOR
                 CHOIR

Scene: A church

Properties: Leaflets

Regular attenders at church sometimes find it hard to imagine people's reservations about coming to a service. Yet many people find stepping into a church rather daunting. They feel uneasy, embarrassed, shy, and even threatened by the unfamiliar surroundings. Similarly, hearing a minister say that he has some "useful leaflets" at the back of the church could present difficulties to some people in asking for them.

A church service finishes and the CHOIR *stand behind the* VICAR. *The choir can actually be the actors from this sketch if there aren't spare people around!*

    VICAR: . . . and if you found the sermon struck a personal note with you I have some leaflets here *(He shows them)* that may help you understand what I was saying. Please ask me for one as you leave. But we hope that you won't be dashing off too soon as we have an excellent bookstall in the porch and invite you all to join us for coffee after the service. Thank you.
        (As he leaves, the CHOIR *leap into action with their song! A tune similar to "She'll be coming round the mountain" fits.)*

    CHOIR: There's coffee and a bookstall at the back. Yes! There's coffee and a bookstall at the back.

There's coffee and a bookstall
Coffee and a bookstall
Oh, coffee and a bookstall at the back.

We'd like to get to know you at the back.
Yes! We'd like to get to know you at the back.
So come and drink our coffee
Please do not be put offee!
For we've coffee and a bookstall at the back.
(The VICAR *is now at the back door to the church.)*

LADY: Thank you, Vicar, a lovely service.

VICAR: Thank you, Mrs Frobisher. Church wouldn't be the same without you sitting in your usual pew. It would be good if you tried mixing with others in the congregation, though.

LADY: No thank you, Vicar. I like my place.

VICAR: Well, Mrs Frobisher, it's really good to see you again. I must call round soon.

LADY: The invitation's always there you know.
*(*LADY *leaves and passes the* GIRL *who now approaches the* VICAR.*)*

GIRL: What a great sermon, Vicar.

VICAR: Well thank you. Would you like one of these leaflets?

GIRL: *(Embarrassed)* Oh . . . no thanks . . .
(She walks away and watches from afar.)

VICAR: *(Perplexed)* Right. Goodbye then.

OLD MAN: Lovely service, Vicar.

VICAR: Well thank you.

OLD MAN: Yes. And that sermon . . . well . . .!

VICAR: One does what one can.

OLD MAN: Do you know that all the things you said really struck home?

VICAR: *(Delighted)* Well, that is the difference between just . . .

OLD MAN: *(Interrupting)* Yes. Each of those points you listed reminded me of someone I know.

VICAR: Ah . . . I see . . .

OLD MAN: *(Leaving)* Very clever . . . thanks . . . yes, very clever that . . . 'bye.

(OLD MAN exits.)

GIRL: *(Rushing up, agitated)* It was a good sermon, you know.

(The VICAR turns to speak but is interrupted by the MAJOR who has the effect of driving the GIRL away.)

MAJOR: You need a new organist, don't you!

VICAR: *(Still looking to GIRL)* Quite possibly.

(To MAJOR) Will you excuse me there's . . .

MAJOR: *(Bashing on regardless)* Timing was all over the place today. Must keep a steady beat you know. *(He beats out a military tune with his stick)* Oh yes. *(He takes the VICAR by the elbow and leads him away for a "quiet word" – one that can be heard everywhere!)* Did she know she had her handbag on the swell pedal or what? You must give her her marching orders you know. Can't have sloppy music in church. Mind you it went with your sermon today – can't give you more than four out of ten for that. And the sooner you go back to real hymns and chuck out this circus music on the guitars the better you'll be. Good day. *(He leaves suddenly.)*

VICAR: I give up.

(The GIRL comes forward again, rather shyly.)

GIRL: I want a leaflet.

VICAR: Certainly. *(He holds one out to her but she does not take it.)*

GIRL: It's not for me, you know, but for a friend. *(She cannot keep her eyes on the VICAR at the moment.)* She's been going through a bad patch lately.

VICAR: Does she come to this church?

GIRL: No. You don't know her. *(Awkward pause)* At least I don't think you know her.

VICAR: Would you like me to meet her or can you cope?

GIRL: No. She doesn't want to talk. She's shy. *(The GIRL can now look at the VICAR)* She . . . she says she wants to know Jesus personally.

VICAR: But she doesn't know where to begin?

GIRL: That's right. I . . . I mean, she . . . sees him only as a name in the Bible. A historical figure. A good man, of course, but still at a distance. I just want to be close to him and accept him into my life.

VICAR: *(Ignoring the* GIRL's *obvious mistake)* Try and find a time to be quiet and be with God. He is waiting for people to accept him, to ask him into their lives. He wants to be with them. With you.

GIRL: He wants to be with me?

VICAR: Oh yes. He stands at the door and waits for us to open it.

GIRL: I'll bet he gets some surprises as he stands at the door!

VICAR: Don't we all! Picture that door with Jesus knocking and remember that the handle is on your side. He is asking to be with you.

GIRL: I'll take this leaflet then . . . and look at it . . . quietly.

(The sketch can end at this point with the GIRL *leaving but it may be more effective and appropriate to use the following action accompanied by the words from Revelation 3.*

The VICAR *passes the* GIRL *the leaflet. Freeze for a moment as both hold the leaflet. The* GIRL *takes it and turns half away. She looks back at the* VICAR *and smiles.)*

VOICE: "Listen! I am standing at the door; if you hear my voice and open the door, I will come in to you and eat with you, and you with me."

The old bag

Bible basis: The widow's offering
Luke 21.1–4

Characters: WENDY, carrying a purse crammed with money
JULIE, wearing a large expensive-looking coat
JAMES
WIDOW
VICAR

Scene: The front pew of a church

Properties: Collection bag

Let's be honest, we all forget things at some time or another. Here is a sketch that shows how three people try and cope with the situation of no offertory just as the collection bag is coming!

The collection is about to be taken. It might be worth having a hymn sung quietly behind the action or have the organist playing in the background to create the right atmosphere. JAMES, WENDY *and* JULIE *are very smart and speak in exaggerated posh accents. The* WIDOW *needs to look poor.*

VICAR: We will now take up our offering for the work and witness of this church. Thank you. *(The* WIDOW *moves out of the pew to get the collection bag and starts passing it along the imagined pews.)*

JAMES: Here comes the old collection bag again.

JULIE: Did you bring the envelope?

JAMES: What? I thought you had it.

JULIE: Why should I have it? You always tell me that you look after the finances.

JAMES: But what shall we do?

WENDY: What's the problem?

JAMES: Julie has forgotten the envelope with our weekly offering in it, that's what.

WENDY: Oh no. But you'll have to pass the collection bag without putting anything in.

JAMES: Thank God it's not a plate, that's all. Everyone at the end of the row would see.

JULIE: I've got some other money with me. We were going to buy a couple of newspapers on the way back. Shall I use that?

JAMES: I said you were no good with finances, Julie. That would mean we'd be giving twice, wouldn't it! We'd have to give the envelope next week, or whenever we come again, because they know what we promised to give each week.

WENDY: Shall I lend you some?

JULIE: Would you? I say that's awfully good of you, Wendy. Isn't that good of her James?

JAMES: Frightfully good of you Wendy. Just fifty pence till tomorrow.

(WENDY *gives him fifty pence.*)

JULIE: Gosh, that got us out of a nasty scrape. That old dear with the bag is nearly at our row.

WENDY: I'm amazed she can carry it all at her age.

(*The* WIDOW *carries the bag along the line. As each character takes it freeze the action so that their "thoughts" can be heard. This could be placed on tape.*)

WENDY: Ah, how good it is to pass on a little of one's wealth to the needy. Though I'm not so sure I shouldn't be giving it straight to this old dear (*She smiles at the* WIDOW.) I'm surprised that they trust her with all this money. (*She peers into the bag.*) Not that those behind have exactly exhausted their wealth, have they! (*She turns round and grins as she produces a bulging purse.*) There, that will make them feel rotten. (*She makes a huge show of placing her five-pound note into the bag.*) No one else has put in any paper money . . . not many of those silly one pound coins either.

WIDOW: Thank you.

(WENDY *is startled.*)

WENDY: Why thank me? I'm only giving the church

some money. Not you. Or do you take a percentage?

WIDOW: Jesus said that the gifts that you give to the poor you'll find you've given to him.

WENDY: But . . . (WENDY *freezes as the bag goes to* JAMES.)

JAMES: When I think of how I actually took the trouble to get those envelopes. That was supposed to make the offering easier to manage. But, oh no, not for Julie here. Trust her to muck it up. And fancy suggesting we use the money for our newspapers. What would we do after lunch, I'd like to know? Listen to the dishwasher spinning round? Sunday wouldn't be Sunday without the newspapers. I don't even miss out the bits about Ethiopia. No, I read it all from cover to cover. Well, perhaps this fifty pence will make a big enough chink in the bag to make them think it's a two-pound coin . . . (*He starts to drop it in the bag*) . . . ah . . . I know . . . knock the side of the bag to make it sound as if it's going in then give Wendy back her money now. Brilliant! No wonder I'm so successful at business. I could teach this old dear a thing or two. She doesn't look as if she's got two pennies to rub together.

WIDOW: Bless you, sir.

(*This startles and perplexes* JAMES.)

JAMES: Bless me? What right have you to . . .

WIDOW: Jesus said that the poor are blessed, for they shall inherit the earth.

(*The bag goes to* JULIE. *All others freeze.*)

JULIE: So who gets to pass the bag without anything to put in it? Muggins again. Why can't he give me some money of my own? If he's so stinking rich, why can't I see some of it sometime? This woman here must think I'm from the Third World if she sees me without any money. How embarrassing! Thank heaven I wore this large coat . . . at least the people behind won't see me pass it on without putting in a jot . . . I mean even one of these buttons would be worth a pound or two but I can't see the vicar cashing it in so I'm not going to waste a perfectly good button in some silly old bag. She can think of me as one of the underprivileged and I don't care.

(The bag is passed back to the WIDOW.)

WIDOW: What Third World?

JULIE: Pardon? You are joking . . . everyone's heard of the Third World . . . haven't they?

WIDOW: In the human sense yes. But God doesn't see it like that. He just sees those who know him and those who don't.

JULIE: Then I'd better . . .

(It is too late, the bag has been taken towards the VICAR. He takes it from the WIDOW and waits while she empties her purse into it. No showing off, no pretences, just a humble offering.)

VICAR ⎫ All things come from you and to you we return
WIDOW ⎭ what is rightfully yours.

WIDOW: With a thankful heart. Amen.

(The music that has been playing now comes to an end. The VICAR leaves with the WIDOW. WENDY walks away, shaken, but trying to put a brave face on things. JAMES looks at the fifty pence still in his hand. He is embarrassed and tries to hide it but drops it with a clatter on the floor. He walks away from the rolling coin. JULIE stamps on the offending coin, pulls her coat around her and leaves.)

Armour getting

Bible basis: The whole armour of God
Ephesians 6

Characters: SALLY $\}$ children's TV presenters
PETER
TOMMY, a wide-eyed boy
CHARLOTTE, a bit precocious
Other CHILDREN
The voice of an ANNOUNCER

Scene: TV studio

Properties: Large box containing:
toilet rolls
egg boxes
silver paper
cardboard box

The message of Ephesians 6 has probably never quite had this treatment! The serious message of God telling us how we should arm ourselves for battle is there and must come across to the spectators within this parody.

The "Playschool" type presenters are really pushing their message home hard and audiences should see the funny side of this method. The presenters accentuate words with actions. SALLY and PETER must act out as many of the words as possible at the beginning. They can "cool off" as the sketch progresses but should still overact from time to time to maintain their characterization. TOMMY and CHARLOTTE are very different in character. TOMMY enjoys and understands make-believe but CHARLOTTE can't partake in it. She is sensible and doesn't want to join in. TOMMY is not outwardly a deep thinker but is by no means stupid.

TOMMY *and* CHARLOTTE, *with others, are watching the new programme being made.*

> VOICE: Quiet please, studio. Ladies and gentlemen, boys and girls, this is a brand new show

we're making for TV. I'm sure you'll join in really well and help "Sunday Playschool" be a great success. It's new, it's exciting and it's ready to go! Places, please, everyone. Good luck all of you . . . three . . . two . . . one . . . go!

("Twee" music introduces the show as SALLY *enters with* PETER. *They are a camel but have no costume to suggest this. After a few turns around the floor they stop when the music does.)*

SALLY: Hello *(She waves.)*

PETER: Hello *(He waves.)*

(They start prancing around again then stop.)

SALLY: Can you guess what we are doing?

PETER: I'm bending like this . . .

SALLY: I'm standing up . . .

PETER: We've got four legs . . .

SALLY: Can you guess what we are?

CHARLOTTE: Really stupid!

TOMMY: A horse?

PETER: No. But we are an animal.

SALLY: We live in a very hot place.

CHARLOTTE: *(With contempt)* A tropical fish?

PETER: No. Hotter than that. A hot, hot place.

CHARLOTTE: A tropical fish and chip shop then?

SALLY: No. You're guessing. Shall we tell them?

PETER: Yes let's . . .

SALLY ⎫
PETER ⎭ We're a camel.

(They troop around again as a camel. It finishes with a silly pose – e.g. legs crossed and hands on chin – something very unlike a camel!)

CHARLOTTE: Camels can't stand like that. They don't have sufficient bones in their forelimbs and anyway . . .

SALLY: *(Quickly interrupting)* Let's dress up as something else.

PETER: I know . . . let's dress someone else up.

SALLY: Who'd like to be dressed up?

CHARLOTTE: Not me!

SALLY: Let's dress Tommy up.

PETER: Let's dress him up as a soldier.

CHARLOTTE: Sexist.

TOMMY: Yeah. Great. Action man. *(He imitates a machine gun and shoots* CHARLOTTE. *She turns away in disgust.)*

CHARLOTTE: Guns are an abomination to people.

SALLY: What can we use to dress him up?

(PETER drags over a large box full of toilet rolls, egg boxes, silver paper, etc. that will be used for the armour.)

PETER: Here's a helmet. *(He shows them the cardboard box he has taken out.)*

SALLY: You need a helmet to protect you from adversity.

PETER: It will be your helmet of salvation.

SALLY: Gosh! Those are big words, Peter. *(To audience)* Can you say adversity?

(All but CHARLOTTE *join in.* TOMMY *is dressed in the helmet.)*

ALL: Ad-ver-si-ty.

SALLY: Good. I know a song about adversity and helmets. It goes like this: *(Tune: "Grand Old Duke of York".)*

SALLY ⎫
PETER ⎭   With a helmet on my head
And a promise in my mind
I'm off to fight adversity
And help all human kind.

And when we are right we are right
And when we are wrong we are wrong
And when we are only half way there
We sing this happy song.

SALLY: Now what else can we give our soldier of Christ?

TOMMY: A gun.

SALLY: Well sort of . . . a shield.

CHARLOTTE: A shield is nothing like a gun!

SALLY: But you carry them both if you are a soldier.

CHARLOTTE: *(With mounting contempt)* Why not a hand grenade then?

PETER: Well that's not a very good idea.

CHARLOTTE: Neither's a shield.

SALLY: Ah, but a shield of faith wards off . . .

SALLY }
PETER } Ad-ver-si-ty.

(Repeat song with the words "With a shield in my hand" etc.)

SALLY: So faith is like a shield. It will protect you from . . .

PETER: . . . the burning arrows of the Evil One.

TOMMY: The what?

SALLY: What Peter means is that we cannot be hurt by the works of the Evil One.

SALLY: Let's arm our soldier with the breastplate of righteousness.

PETER: Great idea. Let's give him a breastplate. *(He rummages through the box. When he finds something appropriate he puts it on TOMMY.)*

CHARLOTTE: Why?

SALLY: Righteousness is at the very heart of God.

CHARLOTTE: What about being happy?

PETER: No. Happiness is not a high enough aim.

TOMMY: A thief might be happy.

SALLY: *(Slightly surprised)* That's right!

PETER: Well done, Tommy.

TOMMY: *(Gaining confidence)* A murderer might be happy.

SALLY }
PETER } Right.

TOMMY: The devil is probably happy too.

SALLY }
PETER } Right.

SALLY: But righteousness is very special.

PETER: Righteousness comes from God.

SALLY: And pleases God.

CHARLOTTE: But *(pause)* . . . OK. *(This latest part has convinced her that it is worth listening at least.)*

TOMMY: *(To SALLY)* Please, miss . . .

SALLY: Yes, Tommy?

TOMMY: Can I always be a soldier of Christ, miss?

SALLY:	Yes you can, Tommy.
TOMMY:	Will I always have to wear these boxes?
PETER:	No, Tommy. They were just used to try and explain what the Bible is saying in Ephesians.
TOMMY:	Don't Christians wear boxes then?
SALLY:	Not normally.
TOMMY:	Then how will people know I'm a Christian?
PETER:	By the things you say and do.
TOMMY:	What should I say then?
SALLY:	God provides us with a mighty weapon to do his work.
TOMMY:	A laser gun?
PETER:	No. Not that. You need something to carve out the word of God, Tommy.
TOMMY:	Hammer and chisel?
SALLY:	No. Not that, but something that will cut through the arguments.
TOMMY:	A saw?
PETER:	No.
TOMMY:	A knife?
PETER:	No.
TOMMY:	A dagger?
PETER:	No. Keep thinking.
TOMMY:	Oh . . . I know.
SALLY ⎱ PETER ⎰	Yes?
TOMMY:	Has it got a blade?
PETER:	Yes.
TOMMY:	Has it got a handle?
SALLY:	Yes.
TOMMY:	Is it in the Bible?
PETER:	Yes!
TOMMY:	It's the axe of apostles.
PETER:	No.
SALLY:	It's a sword, Tommy.
PETER:	The word of God will be your sword.
CHARLOTTE:	So how will a Christian soldier carry all this clobber?
SALLY:	With honesty.
PETER:	With truth.

CHARLOTTE: And a belt?

SALLY: You're right. In Ephesians it describes it as the belt of truth around your waist.

PETER: With the armour of God you cannot be beaten.

CHARLOTTE: What, little Tommy can't be beaten?

PETER: Nobody who is a Christian can be beaten.

SALLY: Jesus' death on the cross saw to that.

PETER: Not even death can beat us now.

SALLY: With the shield of faith, the helmet of salvation, the breastplate of righteousness and his word in the sword we cannot be beaten.

CHARLOTTE: What? Nothing can beat you?

PETER: Nothing at all.

CHARLOTTE: That's incredible . . . and even that belt around the waist?

TOMMY: Oh yes . . . that's the truth!

(They exit talking together – a very friendly group.)

62

A select group

Bible basis: Jesus' choice of disciples
Luke 6.12–16; Mark 3.13–19

Characters: INTERVIEWER
SECRETARY
Twelve "DISCIPLES" (possibly from the audience)
USHER (optional)

Properties: Cards showing disciples' names
Two clipboards with sheets of notes

A similar idea to this has been used in church magazines, etc., but here the scene comes to life in performance. It is a good "ice-breaker" for audiences of all ages. Try and involve the audience whenever you can. In *A Select Group* you have the chance to meet them during the sketch. This makes later contact easier for many people.

This sketch is improved if the TWELVE DISCIPLES are played by members of the group or audience. If you don't have enough people watching then use photographs of the candidates. You need to warm up the audience first. This can be done by getting the audience to name the disciples (sounds like a game show!) and rewarding them with a card to hold showing the name that they called out. Once the warm-up is completed and all twelve are at the front the INTERVIEWER and SECRETARY can start their dialogue. It is often good to point out that the twelve people at the front are as mixed a group as the first disciples were. For one thing they probably don't know each other very well!

Enter an INTERVIEWER: *who approaches the* SECRETARY. *Both hold clipboards and sheets of notes. These will probably be the script!*

INTERV: Good afternoon. Sorry to interrupt, but we're conducting a social survey for the Jordan Government.

SECRETARY: I'm sure we'd be glad to help.

INTERV: We've received a list of nominees from a Jesus

of Nazareth who wishes to create a management team for his father's business.

SECRETARY: Is he the carpenter's son?

INTERV: Well . . . *(Unsure)* yes. I suppose we could call him that. There's always been a question about that . . .

SECRETARY: We keep careful records – I'm sure we can help. Are these the twelve?

(They look at the TWELVE DISCIPLES. *If the audience was too small for twelve to be found then a series of photographs could be passed to the* SECRETARY. *As each is introduced he or she is brought forward, discussed and dismissed. It will probably help to have an* USHER *to do this job.)*

INTERV: Simon.

SECRETARY: Simon? *(He looks through his notes.)*

INTERV: Yes. But he's going to be called Peter.

SECRETARY: Peter. *(He searches again.)*

INTERV: Yes. Simon Peter.

SECRETARY: It'll play havoc with our filing system . . . Ah . . . here we are . . . Simon Peter. Oh dear . . . tut, tut . . . oh dear. He has a bad temper and is emotionally unstable. I'm afraid that . . .

(Exit SIMON PETER.)

INTERV: James and John.

SECRETARY: James and John are brothers and in our experience would probably place personal interest before company loyalty. So . . .

(Exeunt JAMES *and* JOHN.)

INTERV: Andrew.

SECRETARY: No leadership qualities. Not really the sort . . .

(Exit ANDREW.)

INTERV: Philip and Bartholomew.

SECRETARY: *(Searching fruitlessly through notes)* We don't know anything about them! Bit of a long shot choosing a couple of unknowns!

(Exeunt PHILIP *and* BARTHOLOMEW.)

INTERV: Matthew.

SECRETARY: Tax collector!

INTERV: Oh good heavens!

(MATTHEW *is speedily despatched.*)

INTERV: Thomas.

SECRETARY: I've got my doubts about him. His records state that he questions everything. Bad for morale, you know.

(*Exit* THOMAS)

INTERV: James and Thaddaeus?

SECRETARY: (*Consulting notes*) Manic depressives with radical leanings. Shall I go on?

(*Exeunt* JAMES *and* THADDAEUS.)

INTERV: Simon.

SECRETARY: We've had him already. Oh no . . . that was Peter. Simon (*Searches through papers*) Simon . . . Simon! (*Takes* INTERVIEWER *aside*) He's a zealot!

INTERV: (*Understandingly*) Oh (*Pause*) . . . a what?

SECRETARY: A zealot. An urban guerilla . . . plotting to overthrow the occupation. Not the best of choices you'd agree.

(*Exit* SIMON)

INTERV: Last one then.

SECRETARY: Ah . . . now here's one with potential. Ability, resourcefulness, meets people well . . . a keen business mind . . . and he's got friends in high places. Could be useful. Certainly ambitious and responsible.

INTERV: What's the name of this responsible chap then?

SECRETARY: Judas Iscariot.

INTERV: Looks the most suitable – on paper anyway. (*To* JUDAS) Thank you. We'll let you know.

(*Exit* JUDAS)

INTERV: So what do you think of the choice?

SECRETARY: Well frankly it seems Jesus chooses anybody. Goodness knows who he'll pick next.

(*They look at the audience, then at each other before leaving.*)

Temptation

Bible basis: Something to pray about
Matthew 6.13

Characters: Five people
Scene: Room with table and chair
Properties: Large colourful parcel
Newspaper

This sketch is very short and simple, and is done almost entirely as a mime. It can be used on the street, in the church, the youth club or wherever. The audience are involved from the start and they are probably just as interested (tempted) as the actors! In school assemblies it can often be tricky to hold the attention of a sometimes unwilling audience. Sketches such as *Temptation* can work well.

ONE *is reading a paper at the side of the stage.* TWO *enters and makes a great show of putting a colourful parcel on a table, and indicates to the audience that the parcel must not be touched.* ONE *shows a little interest but goes back to his/her paper. Nothing happens for a while other than the occasional glance (at the parcel) from* ONE *as s/he turns over the pages.* THREE *comes in and picks up the parcel, tests its weight and replaces it. S/he shrugs at* ONE. ONE *is now more interested and strolls towards the table when* THREE *leaves.* ONE *looks at the parcel but goes away when* FOUR *approaches.* FOUR *lifts up the parcel and shakes it. S/he gives a knowing nod at the audience and* ONE. ONE *is peeved by this and goes back to the parcel when alone. S/he just touches the parcel before retreating as* FIVE *approaches.* FIVE *lifts up a corner of the wrapping and peeps inside. S/he indicates to the audience that it is something good and goes away pleased at his/ her find.* ONE *throws down the paper and rushes to the parcel, rips it open and reveals its contents – a sign reading "Lead us not into temptation".*

(It might be appropriate, instead of a sign, to have a tape recorder that plays the message over and over again, or to have

ONE read out the sign for the audience. This will depend on the
setting for the presentation. Remember that everyone must
see or hear the punchline.)

Drawing conclusions

Bible basis: The two house builders
Matthew 7.24–27

Characters: MAYOR
MR SCRIBBLING, his secretary
HELEN HIGHWATER, a smart, efficient businesswoman
with persuasive ways
NOAH VALE, a rough labourer with a simple outlook on
life
SEYMOUR CLEARLY, an honest builder
Three NEWSPAPER SELLERS (voices can be taped)

Scene: The planning office of a town council, with desk and
chairs

Properties: Clear building plans – on paper or acetate
Overhead projector (if plans are on acetate)

Although this sketch is based on the story of the house upon
the rock, it also takes a slightly different slant. And not just
because there are three builders instead of two!

The MAYOR *is ready to interview prospective builders and town
planners.*

SCRIB: *(Entering)* Good morning, Mr Mayor.
MAYOR: Oh . . . morning, Mr Scribbling, are the
builders ready to show me the plans?
SCRIB: Yes, Your Worship, they're all here. Shall I show
them in?
MAYOR: If you would please.
(SCRIBBLING *goes to the door as the* MAYOR *arranges
his papers. He shows in* HELEN HIGHWATER.)
HIGH: Mr Mayor, how good of you to see me. I do hope
you like the plans I have drawn up.
MAYOR: Very good of you to come Ms Highwater. Let's
get straight down to business and see what you
have to offer.
(HIGHWATER *starts to get the plans ready for*

viewing.)

HIGH: Well, as you know, sir, my company has always prided itself on buildings of distinction. We cater for a particular kind of client: the young executive, the successful businessperson . . . the local dignitary.

(She smiles ingratiatingly at the MAYOR *who returns a sickly smile, although quite flattered.)*

MAYOR: Of course . . . very good . . . oh, yes . . . very good policy. I certainly approve of your company's taste.

HIGH: And of course there would be substantial . . . shall we say . . . benefits . . . for any local government councillor wishing to purchase a part of the new development.

MAYOR: Goodness, Ms Highwater . . . that could be misread as a bribe!

HIGH: Or an astute business move!

MAYOR: What? . . . Oh yes . . . very astute. Do go on.

HIGH: Well here are the plans of your . . . I mean the new development.

*(*HIGHWATER *unveils the plans. They are very grand and highly detailed. A very smart executive type residence, for example. The* MAYOR *and* HIGHWATER *discuss some of the features.)*

MAYOR: Tell me, what are the foundations like on this property? Are you able to overcome the subsidence problems in that area? It is very sandy where you propose to build.

HIGH: Sandy?

MAYOR: Oh yes. Goodness me . . . the whole area used to be a pit. They only filled it in a few years back. Are you sure that everything would stand firm?

HIGH: I'm sure there would be no problem there, sir. With the latest high valuvium stressed girders and disporigible support struts there would be no problem I assure you.

MAYOR: High valuvium? Disporogioble? You've lost me there I'm afraid, but I'm sure that you know what you're talking about.

HIGH: Oh yes. You can trust me.

MAYOR: Well, Ms Highwater. I think I can say that I am most impressed. Most impressed. I can just picture what the house would be like and will certainly remember your favourable suggestions regarding special discounts for the astute businessperson. Ha, ha.

(They both laugh at this and shake hands.)

HIGH: Mr Mayor, I know you are a fair man and that you will wish to see all my competitors in due course, but can I just say that I doubt if you will find a better offer.

MAYOR: Well we don't know what they have to offer.

HIGH: Mr Mayor, whatever they offer I can beat it. Trust me.

MAYOR: Enough said, Ms Highwater. Thank you again. I'm sure we will be in touch before too long.

HIGH: Thank you, sir.

(HIGHWATER *exits and* SCRIBBLING *shows in* NOAH VALE.)

SRIB: Mr Noah Vale, sir.

MAYOR: *(Under his breath)* Oh no. *(To* VALE*)* Mr Vale. Always a pleasure to see you. Do you have some plans for me?

VALE: Most certainly, sir. Some simply stunning creations from the top team. As you know from experience, sir, we are a family business and work to exacting standards. Here, sir, are the plans drawn up by my youngest.

MAYOR: Youngest?

VALE: Youngest son, sir. What he lacks in age we make up for in quality.

MAYOR: Really? Well perhaps I can be the best judge of that.

VALE: Prepare to be amazed. *(He reveals the plans with great pride and smiles delightedly as the* MAYOR *gazes at the drawing. It is rather like a child's drawing, a playschool house – one dimensional, roughly drawn in wax crayons or felt tip pens! The* MAYOR *stares in disbelief.* VALE *continues to beam. The* MAYOR *looks from* VALE *to the drawing and back several times, unable to find words. He hides his horror quite well! This action should last a while.)* As you can see there is a door *(He points)* . . . and some windows *(He points again)* . . . and a roof. *(He points.)*

MAYOR: *(Shaken)* A roof?

VALE: Oh yes. All our houses have roofs.

MAYOR: All your houses? . . .

VALE: . . . have roofs.

MAYOR: *(Gaining composure)* Obviously I cannot give you a decision right away.

VALE: Of course not, Mr Mayor.

MAYOR: Perhaps you'd like to call back . . . no . . . better still I'll get my secretary to call you in a day or so.

VALE: Well thank you so much, Mr Mayor. I'll be waiting for your call – as they say!

MAYOR: Oh yes *(Aside)* you'll be waiting. *(Calling)* Thank you Mr Scribbling, I'll see the next person if you please.

*(*SCRIBBLING *shows out* VALE *and escorts* SEYMOUR CLEARLY *into the office.)*

SCRIB: Mr Seymour Clearly to see you, Mr Mayor.

MAYOR: Many thanks. Ah, Mr Clearly, how nice of you to call.

CLEARLY: And nice to see you too, sir. I see that you have already met Ms Highwater and have no doubt been tempted by her plans.

MAYOR: Tempted?

CLEARLY: Well I'm sure that her plans were of a very high standard.

MAYOR: Oh yes . . . but of course . . . very high standard. But I've not come to any decisions yet. You know me – I always like to do business in an honest and above-board manner.

CLEARLY: You really are very astute.

MAYOR: *(Edgily)* Astute . . . yes . . . that's right . . . astute.

CLEARLY: Well here are my plans, Mr Mayor. I'm sure that you will approve.

(CLEARLY's plans are as detailed as HIGHWATER's and a similar, though briefer, exchange of comments can take place.)

MAYOR: Well, Mr Clearly, have you given due consideration to the position of this new development?

CLEARLY: My house would be built on a sure foundation. The ground is rock.

MAYOR: But would that be rather pricey?

CLEARLY: True. There would be a price to pay but the benefits would be tremendous. My method would not be the easiest but it would be the most enduring.

MAYOR: Well I don't know. I don't like being rushed into a decision.

CLEARLY: How much time have you got in which to decide?

MAYOR: Well I can't be that sure. I have no idea how much time I have got.

CLEARLY: But it may not be that long?

MAYOR: Possibly not. That's why I'm not sure which plan I should accept.

CLEARLY: Well, Mr Mayor. It is only you who can decide. You have seen the plans and now the choice is up to you.

MAYOR: Mr Scribbling. Could you show Ms Highwater back in?

SCRIB: Certainly, sir.

(SCRIBBLING shows HIGHWATER back into the office. CLEARLY and HIGHWATER stand either side of the MAYOR. SCRIBBLING stands away from the centre of the action. Both builders hold their plans towards the MAYOR who looks from one to the other.)

MAYOR: Now here's a difficult decision. A quick, cheap house built on sand or an expensive version built on rock? Now which is the right decision? It seems pretty obvious to me.

(Both put their plans nearer to the MAYOR. The MAYOR starts to reach for HIGHWATER's. Freeze. Three

NEWSPAPER SELLERS *step into the light and call out their news headlines.)*

NEWS ONE:	Huge floods predicted!
NEWS TWO:	Storms destroy property and leave many homeless.
NEWS THREE:	Mayor's house worst hit.
NEWS ONE:	No compensation for shoddy workmanship.
NEWS TWO:	Mayor's family to sue for damages.
NEWS THREE:	Builder of false hopes flees country.
NEWS ONE:	The house on the rock stands firm.
NEWS TWO:	Mayor's funeral tomorrow.
NEWS THREE:	Future uncertain.

Faithing reality

Bible basis: Faith and actions
James 2.14–26

Characters: CHAIRPERSON/VICAR
Three CHURCH MEMBERS
A STRANGER
Scene: A committee room with chairs

This sketch, one of the earliest by the Lightswitch team, may well be recognized by people who spend their time in committees! It can be a good "ice-breaker" for an audience and certainly gets them involved. If the actors sit amongst the audience then the effect can be even more realistic. The sketch can be concluded with a piece of music or song.

The stranger must have a strong impact on the sketch and must catch the audience's eye whenever s/he appears.

A (church) meeting with a CHAIRPERSON *and three people.* ONE *and* TWO *are standing next to each other.* THREE *and the* CHAIRPERSON *are slightly apart. All the other chairs are empty. The final phrase of a hymn is sung (e.g. " . . . to be a pilgrim") and the congregation close their books.*

CHAIR: Thank you. Well sung . . . well done and well come!

MEMBERS: *(Polite laughter, "Jolly good", etc. They sit while* CHAIRPERSON *the remains standing.)*

CHAIR: Has everyone received the minutes of the last meeting? *("Aye" from* MEMBERS*)* Good. Are they a true record and shall I sign them? *("Aye" from* MEMBERS *again)* Thank you. Now, there is only one item on the agenda today – how to share our faith. *(He looks through his notes, searches for a pen etc., unaware of what others are saying.)*

ONE: What did he say?

TWO: Something about his face.

THREE: What's wrong with it?

CHAIR: *(Continuing)* Now it's a difficult problem and one we must tackle.

ONE: Did he say ankle?

TWO: No, I don't think so. I'll ask. Excuse me. *(Raises hand.)*

CHAIR: Ah. We have an idea already. Splendid. Yes?

TWO: Did you say ankle?

CHAIR: I don't think so. Did I?

ONE: Well it's a bit off the subject.

CHAIR: I would agree. What's that got to do with someone's faith?

TWO: Yes. Of course it is – it's miles from our face.

CHAIR: My face?

ONE: Yes. He couldn't have said ankle. It stands to reason.

TWO: How can an ankle stand to reason?

ONE: Search me. I thought we were talking about faces.

CHAIR: I'm sorry, I think we're way off course.

TWO: Off course?

CHAIR: Of course.

ONE: Of course we're off course.

CHAIR: Please may we start again?

(THREE stands up and starts to sing the hymn again. The looks from the others soon tell him/her that a mistake has been made.)

CHAIR: I didn't mean start right at the start, I meant go back to the front and face the problem.

ONE: Oh you did say face then!

CHAIR: No! Not face . . . faith. F-a-i-t-h. Faith.

ONE: Oh – our faith. *(Turns to TWO)* It's not his face that's the problem.

THREE: That's your opinion.

ONE: I think it's a nice face.

TWO: Yes. So do I.

(ONE, TWO and THREE argue among themselves.)

CHAIR: Order! Order! If I might be permitted to say something.

(ONE, TWO and THREE subside into their places.)

CHAIR: We have inadvertently hit on one of our main

problems. We set out with every good intention of sharing our faith and we are immediately distracted from God's work and follow the wrong path.

ONE: Well, why don't you speak up more?

TWO: Yes. That's another problem. We're afraid to speak up.

THREE: Why don't we get closer together?

CHAIR: Right. Now we're getting somewhere. How can we keep on the right path, how can we speak up more and how can we come closer together?
(As one they move their chairs closer together and look pleased at their progress!)

TWO: What's that got to do with sharing our faith then?

CHAIR: We need to share our faith far more with all those in this town.

ONE: City!

TWO: County!

THREE: Country!

ALL: World!
(Cheers, applause, great celebration, etc., then a long pause.)

CHAIR: How?
(Longer pause. Shuffling of feet, returning to places, looking down, etc.)

THREE: Advertise.
(Others cheer. Ridiculously ecstatic.)

ONE: Newspapers.

TWO: TV.

THREE: Films.
(Cheers again. A STRANGER *enters the scene.)*

ONE: Make an advert . . .

TWO: Yes?

THREE: Make a TV advert.

ALL: Yes!!
(The STRANGER *is now right in their midst but no one notices him/her.)*

STRANGER: Excuse me.

CHAIR: Great!! Let's make a start. Clear a way there.

STRANGER: I was just wondering *(The others rush off)* . . .
what the meeting was about.
(The STRANGER *is puzzled but not put off by their attitude. S/he waits before leaving. The scene changes to a TV studio. This need only be a different part of the acting area. The action should be continuous.)*

CHAIR: Right. Let's have a go. Lights. Sound. Action.
(The acting is incredibly wooden.)

ONE: Yes, it's good to be a Christian.

TWO: It's really good to share *(S/he hands* ONE *a sweet.)*

THREE: And if you'd like to come on down

ALL THREE: You'll really know we care.
(They very awkwardly link arms or shake hands.)

ONE: So come on to our church now

TWO: And join in with the rest

THREE: Here's a special welcome
(They reach out their hands in welcome.)

ALL THREE: That makes our Sunday best.
(They have fixed grins on their faces. They find it hard to keep smiling.)

STRANGER: Hello, my name's . . .

ALL THREE: You've ruined it. What do you think you're up to? . . . barging in here . . .

CHAIR: Cut. Cut. Cut. Can't you see we're making an advert?

ONE: We are trying to share our faith.
(They leave. The STRANGER *remains.)*

STRANGER: I wonder what it is they are trying to advertise.
(S/he leaves, unhurried. After a short pause, ONE, TWO, THREE *and the* CHAIRPERSON *re-enter.)*

ONE: This just isn't working.

TWO: Why don't we try something else?

THREE: Like what?

CHAIR: Look . . . look . . . why don't we make a . . . you know . . . one of those *(he forgets the word billboard)* . . . what do you call them? . . .
(A game of charades now takes place at the end of which a solution is eventually found. The word can be divided into two with a bird's bill and a

bored person.)

ALL: A billboard. Yes! Great idea.

ONE: It will have to be big so everyone can see it!

TWO: It will have to be huge so everyone knows.

THREE: It will have to be enormous.

CHAIR: Great idea. Let's start.

(Much activity – mainly useless – getting paper, paints, brushes, etc. Amidst the worst commotion the group are suddenly aware of the STRANGER who has entered. The chaos subsides.)

STRANGER: What are you doing?

ONE: It's a poster.

TWO: About our faith.

THREE: We wanted everyone to know.

STRANGER: Why don't you just tell them instead?

CHAIR: No adverts.

ONE: No huge posters.

TWO: No films.

THREE: No need.

STRANGER: Let people know by the way you live and every word you say.

(The sketch can finish with a song or the words of John 14.15–17.)

Tempting mortals

Bible basis: The old life and the new
Colossians 3.5–10

Characters: DR STRANGETRUTH, a doctor devil
DAVE, an office worker
SUE, an office worker
TIM, an office worker
LUST, a tempter
HATE, a tempter
ENVY, a tempter
DEVIL ONE
DEVIL TWO

Scene: An office, with desks which have in trays and out trays

Properties: White doctor's coat
Devil's horns
Clipboard
Red telephone
Handkerchief

Audiences seem to enjoy seeing the occasional horned devil but there is a subtle element to the sketch as well. Like *Knock Three Times*, this shows an ordinary scene containing a Christian and highlights the temptations that surround us all. The power of temptation is evident but the victory is clearly won by the good side!

Two people are sitting at the desks, slowly taking from the in tray, doing some work and then passing it to the out tray. To the right of the stage is a devil with horns – STRANGETRUTH in white doctor's coat, holding a clipboard.

STRANGE: Let me introduce myself. My name is Dr Strangetruth and I am the personal tempter of this poor human (*Points to* DAVE) who is suffering from a chronic attack of Christianity. (*Tuts and shakes head*) He's had it for six months now . . . and he just isn't getting worse. He's been good, kind and considerate for the whole time and he goes to church every week! You can't even begin to imagine what it's been like for me . . . it's been hell, if you'll excuse the expression! If I don't shake off the enemy's hold on this one soon . . . well . . . *(Makes motion of cutting throat. Red phone at back of stage rings.* STRANGETRUTH *makes his way to the phone, marked "hot line", picks up the receiver and then drops it.)* Aaaaooowwww! *(Blows on hand and wraps handkerchief round it and picks up the phone)* Hello, Dr Strangetruth – Tempter 4451 here. *(Pause)* Oh! Your Supreme Badness, Your Exquisite Evilness, Your . . . *(interrupted in mid-creep)* No . . . no luck yet, but . . . *(interrupted; tries again)* No . . . no . . . yes, but . . . no . . . perhaps I could request some back-up, . . . yes a devilishly rotten idea, Your Supreme Evilness. Yes, fine. Thank you. *(Puts the phone down)* That was Big D. *(He moves back to the workers)* Now, this goody goody mummy's boy of a Christian won't know what's hit him. Soon he'll be in the deepest depths of depravity. *(He laughs wickedly.* LUST *enters, checking that he has the right office.)* Ah, here comes my helper. Are you Lust?

LUST: No. I know where I am.

STRANGE: Not lost . . . lust. Are you Lust?

LUST: It is I. Where is he then, Doctor?

STRANGE: Here! This one. *(He leads him across to* DAVE.)

LUST: *(Examining* DAVE) Hmmm . . . yes I can see the problem. Still I have an idea. *(Looking at* STRANGETRUTH) That young thing from the typing pool. *(Clenches his fingers.)* *(Enter* SUE.)

SUE: Hi Dave, Hi Tim. *(She smiles at the two men as she walks past and starts filing in front of the desk.)*

LUST: (To STRANGETRUTH) Now watch and learn. *(He goes and speaks in* DAVE's ear.)* Well look at that eh! Did you see the way that she smiled at you when she came in? She likes you. I can tell you know . . . ask her what she's doing at lunchtime.

DAVE: How's your husband, Sue?

SUE: Oh just fine thanks.

LUST: Don't worry about him, Davey, my boy. He'll never know . . . just a little fun, eh? Nothing serious . . . no harm in it really.

DAVE: Whoever God has joined together let no one break apart.

LUST: *(Physically knocked back)* No chance with this one, Doctor. I suggest you ask for Hate and Envy. They make a great double act. *(He leaves.)*

STRANGE: *(Picking up phone)* Hello, Your Supreme Evilness, tormentor of millions of souls. You . . . *(interrupted)* No. I'm afraid it didn't work. The enemy has really got at this miserable human. I was wondering if you could spare Hate and Envy. I hear that they are working together these days . . . thank you, Master, thank you. *(Hangs up and walks to DAVE)* Now we'll see what you're made of!

(Enter HATE and ENVY. HATE speaks in a very aggressive and loud voice.)

HATE: I presume that this is the miserable specimen *(Pointing to DAVE)* that you disturbed my tormenting for?

ENVY: *(To HATE)* It's alright for you – at least you get to torment. All I do is tempt, tempt, tempt but do I ever get to torment souls? Oh no.

HATE: Shut up and get on with it!

(HATE and ENVY take up position either side of DAVE. Play then shifts to SUE, DAVE and TIM. SUE takes a big pile of work and puts it in DAVE's tray and then turns to TIM.)

SUE: Tim . . . the boss asked if you could go to lunch with him today. I think it's about your promotion.

TIM: Thanks, Sue. *(He turns to DAVE and winks)* Well, here we go Davey, my boy. *(He looks back at his desk.)*

ENVY: *(In DAVE's ear. DAVE should react now and be slightly tempted.)* That's right . . . he gets the promotion, he gets to go to lunch with the boss and who does all the work, eh? You! Just look. *(Points at the new pile of work)* You do three or four times as much work as him and he gets all the credit. It just isn't right!

HATE: Stand up for yourself; tell him what you think of him.

ENVY: It just isn't fair.

HATE: Take him outside.

ENVY: Why him and not you?

HATE: Sabotage his work when he's at lunch.

ENVY: If you can't get promotion, why should he?

HATE: Let his car tyres down on the way home.

ENVY: It's not what you know but who you know.

HATE: He's mucked up your chances you know.

ENVY: He told the boss you were no good.

HATE: He's walked all over you.

DAVE: Congratulations, Tim. You deserve it. *(To* HATE*)* Love your enemies.

(HATE *is knocked back.)*

Do good to those who hurt you.

(ENVY *is knocked back.)*

Bless those who curse you and pray for those who ill treat you. *(He looks at his watch)* Ah, lunchtime.

(DAVE *gets up and leaves followed by* TIM *and* SUE. HATE *and* ENVY *get up and start to leave – badly hurt.)*

HATE: *(To* DOCTOR*)* You idiot! You didn't warn us, you incompetent fool. I shall report this.

ENVY: It's alright for you just standing there you know . . . it hurts being hit with the words of the enemy . . . you hear all that truth and justice. *(He shakes his head in disgust and they both leave.* STRANGETRUTH *is facing the audience as* TWO DEVILS *enter.)*

STRANGE: Big D will understand . . . after all, he's not all bad. What am I saying? Of course he's all bad . . . he's the devil!

DEVIL ONE: Big D wants a word with you, Doc.
DEVIL TWO: You know the price of failure!
            (The TWO DEVILS *escort* STRANGETRUTH *off the stage.)*

Knock three times

Bible basis: Temptation
Luke 22.54–62; James 3.1–12

Characters:	PETER
	NEIGHBOUR
	BILL, a salesman
	FRIEND
	WIFE
Scene:	Room with a door and chair
Properties:	Several watches
	Money

It really doesn't matter if the characters are male or female (but it helps!). They are called by these names in the script but in performance it would be good to call them by the actors' names.

The three temptations within *Knock Three Times* cause three denials. The main character didn't mean them to happen. They just did. Isn't that often the case?

When this sketch is used it may be important to bring out the message of forgiveness by using a song, reading or an explanation. A sketch like this often forms just one part of a whole package of drama, music or other media.

PETER *is in the house, doing some everyday sort of job (like ironing, talking to the goldfish, varnishing a chair, etc.) when he is interrupted by the first knock on the door. He opens it and there stands the* NEIGHBOUR.

PETER: Hello there. *(Aside to audience)* Wait for it – all the latest gossip. I mustn't get involved with this. *(Back to* NEIGHBOUR*)* Good to see you.

NEIGHBOUR: Well what do you think of that new family then?

PETER: I don't really know them that well. I saw them in church on Sunday though.

NEIGHBOUR: Well according to Mrs Kirby they got thrown out of their last home. Trouble with the payments, she says . . .

PETER: Well we can all have trouble with paying bills. Perhaps one of them got transferred . . .

NEIGHBOUR: You can't get transferred in his job *(Looks around)* . . . if you get my meaning.

PETER: *(Warily at first)* Why? Is he in a high-security role?

NEIGHBOUR: Oh no *(laughs)* . . . nothing secret about his daily routine . . .

PETER: Why? What does he do then?

NEIGHBOUR: Unemployed you know. Or unemployable!

PETER: But he seemed a decent enough chap when we spoke last weekend.

NEIGHBOUR: Well that just goes to show doesn't it?

PETER: A little rough spoken perhaps . . .

NEIGHBOUR: Really?

PETER: Yes. And I suppose his clothes were a little unusual for this area . . .

NEIGHBOUR: Clothes unusual, eh? I hadn't noticed them myself.

PETER: Well he had an open-necked shirt and the collar was all frayed and there were at least two buttons missing.

NEIGHBOUR: Is that so?

PETER: Yes and I remember remarking to someone – I don't know who – that flared trousers must be making a comeback.

NEIGHBOUR: Flares? Good grief! I thought they were in museums now!

PETER: *(Laughing)* Along with his shoes!

NEIGHBOUR: Well I must take a better look at him next time I go past. Can't stop now . . . don't want to be accused of gossiping do I?

PETER: *(Realizing his role)* Oh no . . . I mean . . . I didn't mean to gossip . . . it was just that . . . *(The door bell rings and the* SALESMAN *is seen. He enters as the* NEIGHBOUR *leaves.)*

SALESMAN: Excuse me, do you have the time?

PETER: No. I'm afraid my watch has broken.

SALESMAN: Then this is your lucky day. Here, have a watch.

(He hands PETER *the watch.)*

PETER: *(Taking it reluctantly)* But that's very kind of you, Bill, how much do I owe you?

SALESMAN: Nothing. The first one's free, gratis, nothing . . . but don't ask me how I got them. Look I've got dozens. *(He shows* PETER *all the watches inside his jacket.)*

PETER: Ah . . . you mean they fell off the back of a lorry?

SALESMAN: You could say that. But I wouldn't ask if I were you. Don't want questions from the docks board do we!

PETER: So you're still working at the docks.

SALESMAN: Yes and no.

PETER: Yes and no?

SALESMAN: Yes I was this morning. No I'm not tomorrow.

PETER: Sacked?

SALESMAN: Slight misunderstanding with the boss. He owes me. He won't pay. I won't work. I can't stay.

PETER: And how does the watch feature in all this?

SALESMAN: Payment in kind, so to speak. How many would you like?

PETER: None. Thank you.

SALESMAN: None? Then what am I to live on? Thin air?

PETER: I'm sorry but if they're stolen I don't want anything to do with them.

SALESMAN: And I thought Christians were supposed to help the poor and needy!

PETER: Well yes we are . . . but . . .

SALESMAN: So you'll give us a few quid for some of these then? *(Offers watches again.)*

PETER: *(Reluctantly)* Well OK . . . just to help you out I'll have a couple.

SALESMAN: Thanks. *(Takes money quickly and gives over a couple of watches, then beats a hasty retreat.)*

PETER: What a day! Gossiping one minute and receiving stolen goods the next!
(The FRIEND *comes in, looking over his shoulder furtively.)*

FRIEND: Peter! I've got it. The one the lads were all

talking about down the pub.

PETER: Eh? Got what? Talking about what?

FRIEND: That video the judges wanted to ban. So it's all fixed up for tonight – round at Kevin's. Bring some beer but don't bring the missus! Got to go.

PETER: But if it's a blue movie . . .

FRIEND: I'll tell you something *(Looks about before speaking)* . . . this is a real classic, mate. You won't be disappointed.

PETER: Well I don't know, what if . . .

FRIEND: What if, what if!! Don't be a wet, get on down to Kevin's tonight. Just for old time's sake . . . for a friend, eh?

PETER: Well OK then . . . I suppose there's no real harm in it.

FRIEND: Well done, Pete . . . see you there. Alone *(winks)*, eh? *(He exits.)*

PETER: *(Not very convincingly)* I'll watch it and use it as a chance to witness.
(Enter his WIFE.*)*

WIFE: You'll never guess what I've just heard.

PETER: Not gossip, I hope.

WIFE: No. Something I've never heard around here before.

PETER: I've had enough surprises for one morning . . .

WIFE: Loud as anything it was . . .

PETER: I've had nothing but gossip, dishonesty and temptation all morning.

WIFE: Well I hope you didn't succumb to any of them.

PETER: What me? Gosh no, of course not. Anyway what did you hear just now?

WIFE: I heard a cock crowing.

PETER: *(Taken aback)* A what?

WIFE: I said I heard a cock crowing, Peter.
*(*PETER *slumps down on a chair slowly – not over dramatically please!)*

Money man

Bible basis: Judas agrees to betray Jesus
Matthew 26.14–16

Characters: JUDAS
Five MEN
Voice of JESUS

Properties: Thirty silver coins
Six torches
Red filter for torch ends (cellophane, etc.)

The scene is sinister, as are the characters of the dark. JUDAS is weak, nervous and easily caught by the trap of the "clever" men. This sketch would therefore pair well with *Ribbons* or *Garments* and the contrast between light and dark would be brought out clearly through its sentiments and feelings. It works best in a space that can be blacked out.

The characters speak in the same order for much of the time so it is important that they stand in a different (random) order. If it is possible to use different levels, then do so as this will add to the overall effect. They can move about as much as they like but this may prove impractical if it is very dark and the stage has blocks, steps, chairs, etc. over it. JUDAS stays in a central position throughout. The whole atmosphere must be tainted by secrecy and suspicion.

Darkness. JUDAS *and* FIVE MEN *enter each carrying a torch. The* FIVE MEN *have six silver coins each in their other hand. Each character shines his torch upwards onto his own face.* JUDAS *speaks in short stilted sentences.*

JUDAS: Are we all here?
OTHERS: Yes . . . aye . . . all here . . .
JUDAS: Have you brought my money?
ONE: I've brought my share.
TWO: Just as we agreed.
THREE: Six pieces each.
FOUR: This had better work.

FIVE: Worth the risk I'd say.

JUDAS: Show me . . . now.

(Each man shines his torch onto the money in his hand. Make it shine and reflect around the area as much as possible.)

ONE: Six pieces each.

TWO: As we said it would be.

THREE: All in silver.

FOUR: Thirty pieces of silver. Correct?

FIVE: Thirty it is.

JUDAS: Good. What do I have to do?

ONE: We've told you. Rid us of this blasphemer.

TWO: You don't sound reliable to me if you can't remember the plan.

JUDAS: Just tell me, will you?

THREE: Take us to him soon.

FOUR: Somewhere not too crowded.

FIVE: Unless it's our crowd of course.

JUDAS: Your crowd?

ONE: As he said – our crowd. You are talking to men of influence here.

TWO: We control this city. We own it.

THREE: If we want a crowd we get one.

FOUR: And on our terms.

FIVE: They say what we want them to say.

JUDAS: So I get him to come to you.

ONE: Alone.

JUDAS: Impossible.

TWO: What?

JUDAS: Impossible, I said.

THREE: Why?

FOUR: Why?

FIVE: Why?

JUDAS: They . . . we . . . keep together, close, like brothers.

ONE: Brothers!

JUDAS: *(Angry)* Yes! Brothers! You don't realize what you want me to do.

TWO: We do. But what about you? Do you realize? He has caused us enough embarrassment!

THREE: Forget it. This man will let us down.

FOUR: But who else is there? We can't let this teacher show us up any longer.

FIVE: Precisely. It's got to be done now. And it's got to be him.

JUDAS: I've said I'll do it, haven't I?

ONE: At a price.

JUDAS: Yes. A price. I'll do it – at a price.

TWO: Stop all this waste of time, will you? I'm risking a great deal meeting at this time and in this place.

THREE: You need to take risks with a man like this.

JUDAS: You can trust me. *(Pause)* I'll do it.

FOUR: Good. Good. When?

JUDAS: Soon. I can't say when. I'll have to get him away from the town.

FIVE: Gethsemane.

JUDAS: Where?

FIVE: It's a garden. It's called Gethsemane.

ONE: Yes. Perfect. Away from the Romans.

TWO: They're not our problem.

THREE: He has friends in all places – even the Roman army.

FOUR: Trust no one, my friend.

FIVE: I agree. Trust no one.

JUDAS: Gethsemane, then. And soon. Leave it to me.

ONE: But you say there will be others with you?

JUDAS: Yes. But I'll manage. I'll lead you to him.

TWO: Right. Are we agreed?

OTHERS: Agreed.

JUDAS: Which one of you will kill him?

ONE: Ah, no. We will not kill him.

JUDAS: You don't expect me . . . ?

TWO: No. Not you. Nor one of us here.

THREE: Just lead our people to him.

FOUR: We will not be there. Or at least no one will see us there.

FIVE: But we will want to know that you do your job properly.

ONE: We are giving you a lot of money, remember.

JUDAS: I'll do it. I will do it.

TWO: You must give a signal to our people.

THREE: We don't want any mistakes.

FOUR: A kiss. Yes. When you see our people near, greet him with a kiss.

JUDAS: I will.

FIVE: Then it is agreed.

JUDAS: Agreed.

ONE: Good . . . good.

TWO: We must be going. This has taken too long.

THREE: Here, Judas. Take your money.

(They each give JUDAS *the coins. Torches shine on the money as it is passed across and remain shining on* JUDAS' *open hands as he holds the coins. The audience need to see the shining money too.* ONE, TWO, THREE, FOUR *and* FIVE *move back slightly and slowly change the colour of their torchlight to red.)*

JESUS: My friend, do what you have to do. If the scriptures are to come true then this has to happen.

Suggested reading

Burbridge P (ed) **Playing with Fire** Marc Europe
Burbridge P & Watts M **Lightning Sketches** Hodder and
    Stoughton
    Red Letter Days Hodder & Stoughton
    Time to Act Hodder & Stoughton
Forde N **One Stage Further** Marc Europe
    Theatrecraft Marc Europe
Grace F **Back to Back's Little Black Paperback Book**
    Kingsway
Lamont G & R **Drama Toolkit** Bible Society
Martin A & Kelso A **Scene One** Kingsway
McDonald A & Stickley S **Drama Recipe Book** Monarch
McIvor N **The Greatest Burger Ever Sold** Minstrel
Scher & Verral **100+ Ideas for Drama** Heinemann
    Educational
Stickley J & S **Using the Bible in Drama** Bible Society
Stevenson G & J **Steps Of Faith** Kingsway
Watts M (ed) **Laughter In Heaven** Marc Europe

Printed in Great Britain by BPCC Wheatons Ltd, Exeter